The Japanese Islands

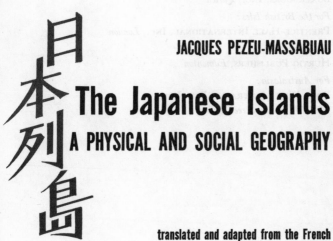

JACQUES PEZEU-MASSABUAU

The Japanese Islands
A PHYSICAL AND SOCIAL GEOGRAPHY

日本列島

translated and adapted from the French

by Paul C. Blum

CHARLES E. TUTTLE COMPANY
Rutland • Vermont : Tokyo • Japan

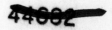

REPRESENTATIVES

For Continental Europe:
BOXERBOOKS, INC., *Zurich*

For the British Isles:
PRENTICE-HALL INTERNATIONAL, INC., *London*

For Canada:
HURTIG PUBLISHERS, *Edmonton*

For Australasia:
BOOK WISE (AUSTRALIA) PTY. LTD.
104–108 Sussex Street, Sydney

*Published by the Charles E. Tuttle Company, Inc.
of Rutland, Vermont & Tokyo, Japan
with editorial offices at
Suido 1-chome, 2–6, Bunkyo-ku, Tokyo*

*Library of Congress Catalog Card No. 77–82140
International Standard Book No. 0–8048 1184–9*

First printing, 1978

Printed in Japan

✦ Table of Contents

5

✦ List of Illustrations

✦ Acknowledgments

I WOULD like to acknowledge the help of the many people who provided me with ideas and material for this book. Living in Japan, I am indebted to the Japanese families that introduced me to their way of life and allowed me to become a member of their households. I am particularly grateful to Professor Kobori in the Geography Department of Tokyo University and to Professor Tanioka of Ritsumeikan University in Kyoto, who, besides sharing their vast knowledge of their country, gave me a great treasure—a warm friendship in a faraway land.

I am also indebted to the many Japanese colleagues whom I met in universities and schools throughout the country and who helped me to understand the geography of their particular regions; especially, Masai Yasuo, Takahashi Nobuhiko, Ogawa Toru, and Sugimoto Shoji. Many of my ideas have come from discussions held with my students and my Japanese friends. I would like to thank them all. Much of the material used in this book was gathered when I was a research worker for the Centre National de la Recherche Scientifique and later

11

when I was a guest researcher at Tokyo University. I would like to express my appreciation to these institutions.

I am also indebted to a number of my countrymen who visited or live in Japan: Jacqueline Pigeot, René de Berval, François Doumenge, Hubert Brochier, Marcel Giuglaris, Augustin Berque, and Jean Waret. I would like to thank the following in Paris: Professors Pierre Gourou, Jean Delvert, Vadime Elisseeff, and the late Professor Charles Haguenauer.

This book was originally written in French, and without the inexhaustible patience of the translator, Paul C. Blum, it would never have been possible.

1

One Hundred Million People
on Twenty Million Acres

WESTERN knowledge and understanding of Japan has long suffered from myths that distance and the little-known origins of the Japanese people have helped to preserve. The quaint and pretty picture painted by many nineteenth-century travelers and the impressions created by the exquisite and colorful works of art they brought back were changed after the Meiji Restoration in 1868 to a picture of a people intent upon military and commercial conquest—people of great sensibility but subject to impulses marked by overpowering ambition. Since the Second World War, yet a third image of Japan is being fashioned by the press, photography, and the film. It is a picture of a peaceful country, skillful and industrious, building upon its cluster of islands one of the world's major industrial powers.

All these images, whatever their degree of reality or unreality, have neglected one important condition of Japanese life, one that has been a major force in the nation's development, especially in recent years: the handicap of overpopulation. This constant menace was not always clearly perceived, nor does it entirely account for

13

the activities that led to the conquest and development of the archipelago. But behind those concerted efforts to develop was the firm determination—displayed only in certain regions at first, then throughout the nation after 1868—to provide a standard of living that would permit the prolific population to subsist.

The bustle and movement today on the plains and along the coast, the "bullet" trains, the huge petrochemical and steel plants erected on reclaimed land—all the prodigious activity that the West observes at times with concern—is but the natural result of centuries of clearing and working the land, of patient efforts to take swamps and mountain slopes and turn them into rice paddies or arable land. During this gradual evolution, techniques were devised that seemed best suited to furnish a means of livelihood for all. Always present, though, were the personal bonds uniting individuals and families and forming them into a national community marked by a cohesion probably unique in the world today.

What are the consequences? Over 110 million people live under conditions comparable to those in certain European countries, in an area amounting to less than 20 million acres. In fact, the lowlands do not exceed this figure, and only by constantly reworking them, employing new techniques according to the needs of the times, have the Japanese succeeded, first in overcoming the problem of overpopulation, then in organizing the first modern consumer's market to be found outside the Western nations. The one country in Asia since the last century to menace the Occident militarily, Japan is today the only one to challenge the economic position of the West while raising the standard of living of its own people at a record rate.

This progress is all the more remarkable in view of the naturally unfavorable (if not actually hostile) environment. The limited extent of lowlands suitable for farming is particularly serious for a people living largely on irrigated rice. The country is ravaged periodically by every natural calamity, either climatic—typhoons, heavy snowfalls, torrential rains, summer fogs, even drought—or of tectonic origin, notably earthquakes. There are landslides, floods, and conflagrations that have been stoically endured for centuries.

Faced with all these dangers, the authorities for a long while felt powerless in the face of their environment. In the sixth century, they borrowed from China—which had already given them Buddhism, the art of writing, and many ideas and techniques—the concept of an all-powerful, semidivine Emperor. The Chinese sovereign, master of the land and the waters, regulator of time and space, intermediary between man and heaven, kept the forces of nature in the proper balance necessary for daily existence by a wise exercise of power and certain propitiatory ceremonies. This concept of power, which the sovereign exercised with the help of men of letters recruited from every class of society by means of an elaborate system of examinations, was soon set aside in Japan. It was replaced by a form of authority that appears to be a fundamental tendency in Japanese society: the ascendancy of certain large and powerful families, bound to each other and to the people at large by strict ties of obligation and dependence. Established on land they had wrested from the Ainu tribespeople of the north and had settled with their dependents and their serfs, these families pursued throughout their great and largely autonomous domains a policy of soil conservation and land

clearance and drainage that reached its full development in the Tokugawa period (1603–1868), two and a
half centuries of peace under a central military government.

Since the Restoration of 1868, a modern government
centralized in Tokyo has assumed these responsibilities.
Imported Western techniques, used with a native ingenuity acquired through centuries of struggle with nature,
have been extremely successful. In the government
ministries in Tokyo, large numbers of technicians are
permanently assigned to investigation and research.
Every aspect of the campaign to conquer the environment of the country is studied: markets, demography, the
drainage of bays and lakes, the establishment of mountain villages, the fight against pollution. Each problem is
carefully considered and the solution judged empirically
before being approved.

Before emerging on a national scale, this intensive effort to use the natural environment and wrest from it a
daily subsistence for all had already appeared at the local
level, in the heart of each region. The Inland Sea provides a good example.

History of a Region: The Inland Sea Basin

The long basin of the Inland Sea is a natural thoroughfare and the most ancient in the land. It is a maritime
thoroughfare, thanks to the numerous islands that fa-
cilitate its use, and also a continental one, because of the
plains that extend the length of both shores—the Honshu
plain to the north in particular. For this reason it was
settled at an early date. But it was not long before the
inhabitants were discouraged by the rocky islands and

narrow coastal plains. From the beginning, they had tried to compensate for the relatively dry climate (the rainfall at the center barely attains 28 inches) by digging pools in which they cached the water needed for transplanting. At the same time, they cut away the hills to form terraced fields, but these proved so barren that the soil often had to be carried up by hand. Arable land had always been scarce; already in feudal times area residents had started to fill in the shallow bays, like the one at Kojima near Okayama. Later they sought to diversify the crops by adding to rice and dry cereals the *igusa*, a reed used in the finest mats, and cotton, which was spun and woven in the home. This soon led to the development of a thriving class of artisans whose work supplemented the region's agriculture and made it possible to commercialize the farm products. They also established breweries for *sake*, a fermented drink made from local rice, and they built many small shipbuilding yards on the islands.

The sea shaped the daily life of the people: it was at once a highway, a place to fish and to collect seaweed and shellfish, and a supplier of salt, which was gathered from the many salt marshes. The sea also offered the chance to escape. In the beginning there were only seasonal departures: ship's carpenters off to seek work in the cities, women looking to sell their mats and cotton goods, salt merchants, stone cutters. However, at first the danger and then the strict laws of the feudal period under the Tokugawa shogunate discouraged these voyages. Moreover, the great fiefs of the region (whose capitals were Himeji, Okayama, and Hiroshima on the Honshu side; Takamatsu, Matsuyama, and Uwajima on the Shikoku shores) were ringed by stout barriers, in theory closing them to all migrants.

According to local legends, a few men from the region dared to undertake the voyage to distant lands. Most travelers, however, set out for places that were nearby and already familiar. They settled permanently in towns they had visited regularly before: Tokyo, Nagoya, Kyoto, and Osaka. For decades the economy of the region showed little change. Then, in 1901, the government built the country's first modern steel mill at Yahata, at one end of the Inland Sea basin. At the other end, the important textile center of Osaka started to expand. Kobe experienced a similar flurry of activity and drew heavily upon the rural population for its labor force. Many of the mountain villages began to empty, and some islands lost almost all of their inhabitants. Only the largest cities, now capitals of the new prefectures and important administrative and commercial centers, retained and sometimes even increased their populations.

Since the Second World War the Inland Sea region has become a part of the industrial belt of modern Japan, and, instead of losing population, it has begun to attract immigrants from the rural areas of central Honshu and the Japan Sea coast. The large industrial companies, finding land unavailable along the Pacific coast, have moved into the area. In many places the shoreline has been reinforced by long concrete walls behind which rise the steel mills and petroleum refineries, while homes for the workers have spread over the adjacent countryside. The Inland Sea itself has become the largest basin for the cultivation of marine life, and the recent extension of the New Tokaido Line bullet trains to Fukuoka via Hiroshima has hastened the development of the region. At the same time, tourism has spread to the islands and to the neighboring shores, causing a proliferation of hotels and the usual tourist trappings. Today the region is no longer in danger of losing its population; it enjoys all the privileges of modern life, and the standard of living of the inhabitants is rising rapidly.

The development of the Inland Sea effectively illustrates a region's response to the complexities of the natural environment through (a) land reclamation, (b) emigration, and (c) absorption of rural population through industrialization. In addition to these three responses, the island country has exercised a fourth alternative: population control.

The Search for More Land

Since most of the Japanese live on narrow coastal plains flanked on one side by mountains and on the other by water, they have from early times sought to encroach upon the sea in order to increase the amount of exploitable land. Many of these plains lie at the head of rather shallow bays that are easily drained by modern facilities. Reclamation projects were first undertaken in feudal times, and old maps show the successive inroads made on bays like the ones at Ariake in Kyushu or at Kojima near Okayama. At Kojima the work was started by a local feudal lord (*daimyo*), revived as a private enterprise in the Meiji period, and is being pursued today with government assistance.

In Niigata, on the Japan Sea coast, we find the earliest evidence of sea drainage. At one time in the region, there were large lagoons which the rural population, lacking adequate means, was unable to reclaim. It was a task that could be undertaken only by a local daimyo since he controlled the necessary labor and capital. Vast areas

were eventually converted into rice fields. One consequence was the formation of large estates that have survived longer than those in any other part of the country.
These settlements can still be found along the coast—the
rural cottages aligned on sandy ridges and forming long
villages; at the center, the home of the leading landowner
rises above the rest while all around extend the empty
paddies.

Later the many lakes and ponds found in every region
were drained. The largest project of this kind was the
Hachirogata lagoon, close to Akita and the Japan Sea
coast, where 88 square miles were totally reclaimed in
1966. Of this great expanse, some 33,000 acres were
given over to rice fields; nearly 8,000 families residing in
the surrounding area were allowed to increase their holdings, while another 800 families were settled on the actual
reclaimed land. Not far from Akita, the slopes and terraces of Mt. Iwate were cleared for use, in part as
pasture land, and here another hundred or so families
were settled. In the meantime, in other parts of the
country, interest in cattle raising led to the clearing of
terraces and uplands which, until then, had been allowed
to grow wild. A number of repatriated colonists from
Korea and Manchuria were resettled in mountain villages
(Tenjimbara, for example, on the Izu Peninsula, south
of Tokyo), where they are now raising cattle and supplying milk to the cities on the plains below.

The development of the eastern region of Hokkaido
was another successful venture. This is the most forbidding area in the entire Japanese archipelago. Arctic in
winter and buried under snow until late spring, during
the brief summer growing season it is blanketed by fogs
that are fatal to rice culture. As a consequence, the hardy

colonists who have settled on the rugged soil of the Kon-sen plateau have turned to dairy farming. However, to support them, substantial help from the government has been necessary in the form of loans for housing and capital investments.

This vast effort to increase the amount of arable land is actually the least spectacular side of the country's desperate struggle to enlarge its territory. For while these new acres are being preempted by the farmer, urban development is eliminating the paddies on the outskirts of the cities, especially along the Pacific coast and the Inland Sea. It is the industrialist rather than the farmer who is land-poor in Japan, and the biggest drainage projects today are being undertaken by prominent companies, who are building polders along the seafront on which to erect their factories.

Above all, the metropolis is steadily encroaching upon the sea. Tokyo, Nagoya, Osaka, Hiroshima, and Kitakyushu, between their commercial centers and their harbors, are feverishly developing a maritime belt that is already a forest of tall furnaces and cracking towers. But even this is not enough; all along the industrial belt, from Kashima north of Tokyo to the Straits of Shimonoseki, the shoreline is disappearing from the map and the natural landscape is being replaced by gigantic industrial complexes bearing such names as Mizushima, Yokkaichi, and Iwakuni. More than ever before, Japan is making an immense effort and sacrificing huge sums in the quest for more land.

The Urge to Emigrate

As Japan's population rose above the 30-million mark

after 1870 and as more and more people sought jobs and dwellings in the cities, the urban areas began to show evidence of the overcrowding we still see today. Some, therefore, sought new frontiers outside the traditional country-to-city migration path.

Where did these people go?

NORTHBOUND

At first, lured by skillful propaganda, they moved to the neighboring island of Hokkaido. Although kept apart for a long time from the other three main islands and isolated by its snows, its fogs, and its immense forests, Hokkaido, even in the Middle Ages, was known to the early settlers in the Tohoku region (northern Honshu). Later, during the Tokugawa period, the authorities established the Matsumae clan on the southernmost tip of the island to contain the Ainu and maintain a beachhead. For a long while thereafter, only a few fishermen were attracted to the island.

But when Vladivostok was settled in 1860 and the Slavic menace to the area became real, the government decided to occupy the island systematically.

It began by sending soldier-settlers whose duty it was both to clear the land and to defend this newest addition to the Japanese island chain. These men drained the swamps, built a solid network of roads across the wide plains at the center and in the east, and founded a new capital, Sapporo. Following them from the poorest areas of the archipelago came farmers attracted by the financial aid the government was offering. Particularly numerous were families from the shores of the Japan Sea and from nearby Tohoku; they established communities that retained the character of their native villages. But nothing in these new surroundings reminded them of their former homes, and the severe climate soon discouraged a great many. In some years the departures were more numerous than the arrivals; today, though most of the island is open to settlement, the population density still remains less than 180 inhabitants to the square mile, as against 705 for the entire country. This number, limited though it is, is sufficient to assure a reasonable development of the island, whose distinctive products give it a special place in the national economy. The wealth of the island—timber (paper), coal and certain metals, pasture lands and cattle, and agricultural products common to a temperate zone (potatoes, sugar beets, wheat)—seems already to have found the optimum density of population for proper exploitation.

BEYOND JAPAN

Those who wished to leave the main islands were faced with certain difficulties, primarily of a psychological nature. The Japanese is deeply attached to his native land; he hates to emigrate, and even to settle in Hokkaido was akin to expatriation. He felt even more hesitant about Hawaii, which was also attracting him, and about Taiwan, Korea, and Manchuria, which Japan had conquered between 1895 and 1932. For a number of reasons, the government soon gave up the idea of turning these territories into populous colonies, and Greater Japan absorbed only a small fraction of the population increase that marks those years.

Nevertheless, those distant lands were essentially still Japan; in them the emigrant could find the civil servants, the language, the newspapers of his own country; there he could live in a Japanese house and be served his native food in the restaurants. He was master; if not always respected, at least he was feared and obeyed. Elsewhere in the world things were different. Australia, North America, and South Africa were prejudiced against Asians not so much because of the color of their skin as because of the danger they were thought to represent. These young nations were intent upon building up their own economies, and they feared a people who demanded so little, who were skillful, hardworking, persevering, and whose simple needs were a threat to native labor. For this reason the history of Japanese emigration is full of frustrated plans and humiliating defeats.

In certain countries—particularly in Brazil—this was not true, however. Brazil was a traditionally hospitable nation where whites and blacks, the yellow races, and the autochthonous Indians had been living side by side on relatively good terms for a long time. Around 1908 the first Japanese immigrants arrived, and by the 1930s they were pouring in. To the already strange racial mixture they merely contributed another strain. The Japanese soon earned a special place for themselves in Brazilian society by their hard work and their spirit of enterprise. Most of them turned to agriculture; some took up the rice culture of their ancestors; others grew tea or cotton on farms they had acquired along the inland railway lines, especially around São Paulo. The city itself absorbed a certain number, some as market gardeners on the outskirts, others as merchants or as representatives of Japanese commercial houses.

Although they appear to have become assimilated, accepting Brazil as their homeland and looking upon Japan as a foreign country, the Japanese emigrants have retained something that is both their strength and their weakness. They have deliberately set themselves apart from their fellow citizens and have revived in this distant land a great many of the ties that united them at home. Their clubs and associations bind them closely, and the old hierarchical patterns, copied from the traditional organization of Japanese society, give them exceptional cohesion. Up to 1945 they accepted wholeheartedly the ideological propaganda emanating from Tokyo, and to this day are definitely more "Japanese" than they will admit.

Within the history of the Japanese people, the period of overseas migration was a very short one, and migration was never an effective means of relieving the pressure on overpopulated areas. In 1940, at the end of the most intensive migration period, the total number of Japanese living abroad was estimated to be 1.7 million; another 1.7 million lived in outlying parts of the Japanese Empire. This 3.4 million was barely four percent of the nation's total population.

Today, although the Japanese are traveling abroad in record numbers for business and pleasure, overseas migration has nearly ceased. The number of settlers in Brazil, for example, was estimated to be 300,000 in 1973. Because of Japan's economic progress at home, fewer people sacrifice family and social ties to seek greener pastures elsewhere. Each year the emigration agencies have fewer applicants, and early requests are often canceled.

Industrialization and Foreign Commerce

At the beginning of the Meiji period feudal barriers were removed and the whole country was opened. Before long, railways were built, relieving the pressure in the rural areas by allowing the excess population to move from the farms to the cities. Everywhere younger sons left home and made their way to the big cities on the Pacific coast where industry and the new commercial and administrative activities were concentrated.

That industry could absorb this surplus rural population was due, in a sense, to the help provided by the world outside. Large numbers of the new city dwellers worked in factories that produced for export. Exports were indispensable because they paid for the raw materials, textiles, and machinery Japan was lacking and helped to redeem foreign loans. In this manner the country was able, almost from the beginning, to develop its industry, take care of its excess rural population, and improve the general standard of living.

Thwarted in their colonial ambitions and obliged after 1945 to return to the narrow confines of their archipelago, the Japanese again turned to industry and urbanization for a solution to their overpopulation problems. Work had to be found quickly for the colonists, the soldiers, and the civil servants. The nation began to look in earnest for foreign markets; in the underdeveloped areas of the Third World, it proceeded to acquire an increasing share of the trade, both as supplier and client. But Japan set out to capture markets in the highly developed industrial nations as well, and its products, from the most simple manufactured articles (textiles) to the most intricate (cameras, electronics) are sold today in every corner of the world. Japanese can also be found building factories, advising industrial planners, constructing dams, providing technical expertise, and furnishing capital all over the world. Japan's varied economic interests are like a vast puzzle in which few spaces in the world have been left blank, and they mark Japan as one of the great producers of wealth of the twentieth century. All these activities are concentrated in the narrow industrial belt that supports the basic economic life of the country and gives work to greater and greater numbers drawn from the rural regions.

Population Control

Emigration, moving to the city, developing a cottage industry—all of these classic means of controlling overpopulation in the countryside were known and practiced from ancient times, as the example of the Inland Sea has shown. Even birth control was practiced before the twentieth century. A cursory examination of population figures for old Japan reveals a remarkable stability: there was an increase of only some 30 million people from the early eighteenth century to the beginning of Meiji 150 years later, in spite of a natural birth rate that probably exceeded the death rate.

It would be easy to attribute this stability to Japan's stagnation, which in turn was due to the deliberate policy of seclusion that cut the country off from all profitable contacts with the continent as well as from foreigners, missionaries, and merchants. However, we must not forget that these population figures were stabilized largely by the common (although officially forbidden) practices of infanticide and abortion. This "pruning," performed to solve the problem of large families, led to the sacrifice in some families of all the children except the eldest son, who was needed to perpetuate the family name. There were some attempts, astonishingly modern in concept, to oppose these practices. As early as the seventeenth century the feudal lord of Sendai, Date Masamune, established in his fief what today would be called family assistance. This was a strictly local project, however, that lasted only a short while and had little influence.

/ Following this long and stagnant period, modern Japan, beginning with Meiji (1868), enjoyed an unprecedented increase in population—from about 33 million to 73 million by 1940. The main reasons for this great increase were the inevitable changes brought about by industrialization: a decline in the death rate as a result of medical and hospital programs copied from the West; a rise in the standard of living in the cities due to the development of a large labor market; and the relative improvement of living conditions on the farms. An important factor was the systematic support furnished by a government most eager to appear to the Western powers (whose threats to the Far East were only too apparent) as a well-integrated, populous industrial nation capable of self-defense.

By 1920, however, the number of births had declined slightly, and although the death rate continued to drop (from 19.2 per 1,000* in 1925 to 16.2/1,000 in 1940), the natural increase rate kept falling, registering 15.6/1,000 in 1925 and 12.7/1,000 in 1940. Nevertheless, the population continued to increase. Many explanations for the growth in population can be found in the post–World War II activities.

The end of World War II brought about many changes. The country had to absorb almost 6 million nationals who had been expelled from its former colonial possessions or who had returned from the battlefields. Concur-

*Hereafter 19.2/1,000.

BIRTH AND DEATH RATES
Total population since Meiji

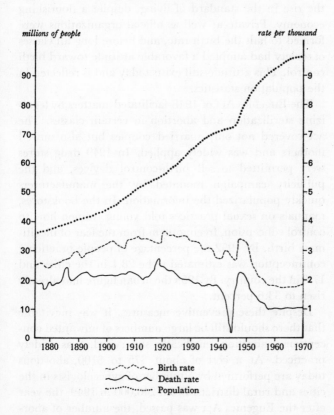

-·-·-·-·- Birth rate
⌢⌢⌢⌢ Death rate
··········· Population

rently, the return of these men resulted in a baby boom that raised the birth rate by 1945 to 34/1,000, while the death rate continued to decline from 16.2/1,000 in 1940 to 7.8/1,000 in 1955. This caused the population figures to rise between 1945 and 1950 from 72 to 83 million.

Such a rapid increase gave considerable concern to economists and sociologists because it acted as a brake on the rise in the standard of living, despite a flourishing economy. Private as well as official organizations were formed to halt the birth rate, and before long all classes of society had adopted a favorable attitude toward birth control. This attitude still exists today and is reflected in the population statistics.

The Eugenics Act of 1948 facilitated matters by legalizing sterilization and abortion in certain classes. The act covered not only married couples but also unwed mothers and was widely applied. In 1949 drug stores were permitted to sell birth-control devices, and the publicity campaign mounted by the manufacturers quickly popularized the information. In the bookstores, manuals on sexual practices told young women how to control conception, freeing them from the fear of illegitimate birth. By 1952 the percentage of people practicing contraception was estimated to be 28.1 in the cities and 17.6 in the country. By 1955 the urban figure had already risen to 33.6 percent.

Despite these preventive measures, it was inevitable that there should still be large numbers of unwanted conceptions; abortion, medically supervised, was widely practiced. At a cost of about $75 to $100, abortions today are performed by a number of gynecologists in the cities and rural districts. From 246,000 in 1949, the year after the Eugenics Act was passed, the number of abortions rose to 1.2 million in 1955 and is estimated today to be 2.5 million a year. The ratio of abortions to births went from 1:10 in 1949 to 6.7:10 in 1955, and today it is over 1:1.

The result has been a decline in the natural increase

rate from 12.7/1,000 in 1940 to 11.6/1,000 in 1955 and 9/1,000 in 1968. For the first time, the normal increase in population has fallen to less than one percent over a period of five consecutive years (1955–60). The population continues to grow but now does so very slowly. If present birth rates continue, the population will reach 130 million by 1990, after which it will decline.

The average age of the population is increasing from year to year, however, and the Japanese economy has felt the shortage of young labor for some time. In the face of this situation, the government is trying to modify public attitudes toward birth control and to tighten restrictions on abortion. Public opinion, however, has not supported such changes so far.

A Higher Standard of Living

Once so numerous that it was unable to feed and house itself adequately, the Japanese population today not only has everything it needs but also strives to attain a standard of living befitting its position in the world. The goods manufactured for export are of secondary importance today; more and more the Japanese factories are devoted to supplying the enormous and very modern domestic market.

Japan ranked third in 1970 in world steel production and third in gross national product, but it still lags behind other modern nations in per capita income, which, at the end of 1970, was estimated to be equal to Italy's. However, a major portion of the wealth produced actually remains with those who produced it, and the rise in salaries and prices, the almost total disappearance of poverty, and the constant effort to modernize public and private life are evidence that Japan has reached a new stage in its pursuit of affluence. The struggle to find work and the bare necessities of life has given way to a search for material comforts.

Remarkable results have already been attained. On the farms, however remote, there are abundant signs of domestic comfort: televisions, refrigerators, automobiles, domestic gadgets of every sort. In the cities, brilliantly lighted thoroughfares that challenge comparison with urban centers anywhere in the world plainly show how far the country has progressed in the last hundred years and, more particularly, in the past twenty years. In the age-old war against overpopulation, here is clear evidence of victory.

This, then, is the central reality in the story of Japan's development: a people for centuries too numerous for the available resources but able, finally, to overcome their handicap by subduing an eminently hostile environment. While the prosperity of the country depends in part upon securing markets and raw materials abroad, it is essentially from their four small and rugged islands that the Japanese people continue to derive their strength. From the narrow confines of these islands, no larger than the Aquitanian basin of France, Japan threatens the foreign markets of the wealthiest nations of the world, yet has managed at the same time to raise the standard of living of its own people.

It is these islands that we shall try to describe briefly in the pages that follow. Highly complex, they offer landscapes composed of ancient paddies and open fields alongside the most modern examples of industrial technology. Contrasts in landscapes and in ways of life and thought are evident everywhere: in agriculture, where swing-plows and burnt-over scrub have not been entirely supplanted by tractors and chemical fertilizer; in manufacturing, where industry is more indulgent than in any other modern country and tolerates the presence of craftsmen still faithful to tradition, and where old-fashioned cottage industry and the small workshop exist in the shadow of immense industrial combines; and in commerce, where the great financial and commercial enterprises accept the competition of small companies that still employ the business methods of an earlier day.

The adoption of today's values and techniques has not automatically resulted in the rejection of those of the past. Many old traditions still regulate human relations even in the most modern enterprises; before a new procedure or a new idea is adopted it is submitted to long and minute study in which centuries of experience and years of empirical practice are brought to bear. In a somewhat similar spirit, we will survey the major aspects of Japanese geography, beginning with the naturally hostile environment that man has encountered in the archipelago.

2

An Inhospitable Environment

ASTRIDE the large, unstable belt of the earth's crust known as the Pacific "Ring of Fire," insular, unprotected, and buffeted by winds that sweep in from the ocean or the Japan Sea, Japan has a most precarious environment. It is essentially a mountainous country whose slopes are constantly ravaged by rains and torrents, while sharp seasonal changes are responsible for heavy snowfalls, droughts, tropical heat, and some of the heaviest rainfall in the world. Japanese civilization was born amid these unbridled elements and bears their marks. While man sought to develop the land, grading it or patiently irrigating it, nature pursued her own work, building here, destroying there, at the mercy of blind forces erupting from the depths of the ocean or the bowels of the earth. In the face of these severe handicaps, the Japanese developed their strength and power.

Mountains, Plains, Shores

Compared with the plains or plateaus of continental Asia, the Japanese archipelago is a recent arrival on the

34

Far Eastern scene. It appears on the map as one of the concave arcs, facing west, that lie off the shores of Asia and extend from Kamchatka to Vietnam and the Philippines. To be precise, it appears where six arcs intersect to form three great nodes: Kyushu (the southwest and Ryukyu arcs), Chubu or central Honshu (the northeast, southwest, and Ogasawara or Bonin arcs), and Hokkaido (the northeast, Sakhalin, and Kuril arcs). Determining the origin of these islands still poses many problems. It is generally agreed that they are of recent formation, appearing in the Tertiary and Quaternary (Cenozoic) ages as a result of a rapid succession of uplifts and subsidences that even now have not ceased. The rock formation dates in part from an earlier age and geologists describe it as (a) a surface shaped by erosion during the secondary period into flat folds or drifts that were later metamorphosed as a consequence of granitic intrusions; and (b) material from the Tertiary period which accumulated to the east of this eroded surface and which was also metamorphosed and uplifted. The oldest zone, in the west, no longer bears a trace of these folds but they are still found in the east in the form of long, parallel, appalachian ridges, which are also particularly prominent in Shikoku and Kyushu.

The land formation everywhere is clearly of tectonic origin. A longitudinal movement formed the Inland Sea trough and the Kansai plain, which is the prolongation to the northeast. In Tohoku, dislocations run north and south from the boundaries of depressions that are separated by almond-shaped mountains. There are faults almost everywhere, breaking up the land into great blocks that constitute the principal mountain ranges, and into depressions in which numerous lakes—Lake Biwa is an example—have formed. The largest of these faults, the "Fossa Magna," traverses the main island of Honshu where the northeast, southwest, and Ogasawara arcs meet; it is marked by majestic volcanoes like Fuji and Asama. Lesser volcanoes rise along the other unstable axes of the archipelago. This active geological past has left the country with more mountains than plains.

MOUNTAINS

It is estimated that four-fifths of the Japanese archipelago is mountainous. More correctly, three-quarters of the land surface consists of slopes of over 15 degrees. However, the terrain in the different regions varies and is of three types. First, there are the rather massive mountaintops generally covered by thick forests; they extend across the four main islands and are a feature of most of the landscape. These mountains never rise above 5,000 to 6,000 feet and present a somewhat monotonous profile despite their abrupt rise from the plains. Deep valleys, often forming straight lines when following some fracture, penetrate the ranges almost to the summits.

In the center of Hokkaido and especially in Honshu, south of the Fossa Magna, a whole world of pointed ridges, sharp peaks, and steep slopes defines a second type of mountainous terrain. The Japanese Alps (Hida Mountains) extend from north to south over a distance of 60 to 70 miles and can boast of about 15 peaks that exceed 10,000 feet. Snow lingers here late into the spring, and the mountainsides are streaked by fallen rocks; however, true glacial forms do not appear to have developed fully in the archipelago. The cascades, fed by melting snows almost until summer, carry down enormous boulders that pile up into steep cones on the sides of the depressed basins that are ringed by these tall, rugged mountains.

The volcanoes provide the third most specific and most varied type of mountainous terrain. Of the 265 known volcanoes, some 20 have been active since the beginning of this century. They are particularly numerous in Hokkaido, the Fossa Magna, and Kyushu (where the arcs intersect) and are few or unknown in the intermediate zones. Their shapes are extremely diverse and show evidence of a long and active history, one that is still incomplete. The mountainous area of Kyushu is one vast lunar landscape: wide craters, at times concealing a lake; great stretches of volcanic ash of every type, gray or black; absence of vegetation; and cones of every form. It is these cones that indicate the proximity of a volcanic zone, be it the perfect ash cone of Fuji, whose 12,460 feet overlook the ocean, the more pointed one (formed of acid lava) of Asama, or the complex and blunter cone of Chokai on the shore of the Japan Sea near Akita. In Hokkaido, the enormous volcanic dome of Daisetsu wears a heavy cap of snow from October to April.

PLAINS

Though plains cover only 16 percent of the country, they must be studied carefully, since the essential activities of man are concentrated there. Unlike the London and Paris regions, these are not basins of sedimentary deposits but depressed zones in which great masses of alluvium have accumulated. The classic Japanese plain has a fairly level profile, sloping rather steeply to the sea where it ends in a line of dunes. Steep heights surround it on three sides, while a swiftly flowing river cuts through the center. Sometimes it lies inside a mountain range, where it assumes an oval or rectangular shape.

The dimensions vary considerably. The extensive coastal plains that border the Japan Sea (those of Niigata, Kanazawa, Izumo) and those on the Pacific littoral, the largest in the country, particularly the Kanto (2,700 square miles) and Nobi (Nagoya) plains, are exceptional. Included in this group are the great plains of Ishikari and Tokachi in Hokkaido. These are large and perfectly flat expanses that stretch to the horizon and on which roads and rails extend in straight lines for miles. Wide river beds lined by high banks cut across these lowlands, which must be drained often and with great effort and which still bear the traces of former streams and meanders. In every region, ascending terraces are a familiar feature of the interfluvial areas; dominating the plains from slightly elevated embankments that are sometimes wooded, they form wide, flat areas through which the rivers have channeled their way. On the approaches to the mountainous areas the slopes steepen and are laced by numerous water courses, sometimes isolating a group of hills that look like steps to the heights beyond. These terraces are a characteristic feature of Kanto; around Nagoya, however, the landscape consists primarily of lowlands that are subject to floods.

Many plains are found in the interior, particularly in the mountainous region of central Honshu known as Tosan. These enclosed basins (Kofu, Nagano, Lake Suwa, Matsumoto) are surrounded by very steep slopes at the foot of which rises a series of sharp and sometimes coalescent alluvial cones that are streaked by mountain torrents. Approaching the center, the alluvium gradually changes from gravel and pebble to sand and mud, providing concentric zones of vegetation and arable land. The torrents follow the slope of the plains, issuing from a

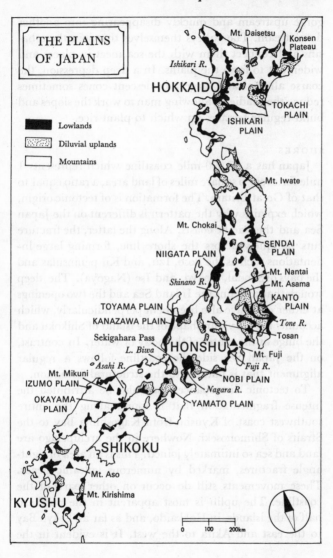

THE PLAINS
OF JAPAN

Lowlands

Diluvial uplands

Mountains

Mt. Daisetsu

Konsen
Plateau

Ishikari R.

HOKKAIDO

TOKACHI
PLAIN

ISHIKARI
PLAIN

Mt. Iwate

Mt. Chokai

SENDAI
PLAIN

NIIGATA PLAIN

Mt. Nantai

Shinano R.

Mt. Asama

TOYAMA PLAIN

KANTO
PLAIN

KANAZAWA PLAIN

Tone R.

Sekigahara Pass

Tosan

L. Biwa

HONSHU

Mt. Fuji

Asahi R.

Fuji R.

Mt. Mikuni

NOBI PLAIN

IZUMO PLAIN

Nagara R.

OKAYAMA
PLAIN

YAMATO PLAIN

SHIKOKU

Mt. Aso

Mt. Kirishima

KYUSHU

0   100   200km

gorge upstream and quickly disappearing into another downstream. The valleys themselves that join these basins and connect them with the sea meet in places and widen out to form the plains. In a deep depression, the coarse alluvial and largely coalescent cones sometimes reduce the gradient, allowing man to work the slopes and build regular terraces on which to plant rice.

SHORES

Japan has a 17,000-mile coastline which represents 1 mile for every 5 square miles of land area, a ratio equal to that of Great Britain. The formation is of tectonic origin, which explains why the pattern is different on the Japan Sea and the Pacific coasts. Along the latter, the fracture cuts obliquely across the shore line, forming large indentations such as the Boso, Izu, and Kii peninsulas and the bays of Sendai, Tokyo, and Ise (Nagoya). The deep trough that contains the Inland Sea and the two openings at either end have also been bent perpendicularly, which accounts for the violin shape of the island of Shikoku and the bulge at the center of the body of water. In contrast, on the Japan Sea side the coastline follows a regular alignment that is parallel to the structural formation.

To tectonic disturbances may also be attributed the intense fragmentation that is found along the entire southwest coast of Kyushu from Kagoshima Bay to the Straits of Shimonoseki. Nowhere in the archipelago are land and sea so intimately joined. This is an area of right-angle fractures, marked by numerous volcanic peaks. These movements still do occur on other parts of the coastline. The uplift is most apparent in the northern half of the islands, in Hokkaido, and as far as Tokyo Bay to the east and Akita to the west. It is evident in the raised terraces, recently eroded again, in the cliffs still unmarked at their base, and in the well-worn plains, the largest of which, the Konsen in southeast Hokkaido, has also again been seriously eroded and fragmented. Here the plains are generally small and sharply tilted. In the southwest, on the other hand, it is the land that has subsided and been invaded by the sea. The borderlands of the Inland Sea and the ria coasts of Kyushu with their numerous islands are evidence of the intensity of the movement. Between these two regions, uplift and subsidence alternate. A good example of the latter is Nagoya Bay where the Nagara and Kiso rivers in no way compensate for the depression, despite the considerable alluvial deposit.

Thus, all along the coastline the two types of terrain alternate. The flat shores often terminate in dunes, notably along the Japan Sea, and are separated from the actual plains by lagoons. In the neighborhood of Tottori, in the San-in region, the dunes cover an area of 15 square miles. The rivers of the region have to flow parallel to the coast for a great distance before they can empty into the sea, affecting the sites of such agglomerations as Akita and Niigata. Cliffs predominate on the Pacific side where they were shaped by fractures into capes and small bays, the form depending upon the basic rock formation. But even here, flat shores are not uncommon and are found at the head of the principal bays (Tokyo, Nagoya, Osaka on the Inland Sea) where the great metropolises are situated. North of Tokyo Bay, the delta of the Tone River presents a type of landscape found elsewhere in the archipelago and which the Japanese call "land of water" (*suigo*). Here the plain is exactly at mean sea level and must be protected by levees and locks as well as by a system of pumps. The river water flows through a network of canals that act as thoroughfares, serving the farmers who can get to their fields only by boat. Reeds and willows lend a kind of Dutch charm to this amphibious landscape.

NATURE'S HAZARDS

These plains, on which the entire population must live, are not only narrow but extremely hazardous, for they are subject to earthquakes and subsidences. The mountains of the region are also unstable, dangerous at times because of the volcanoes and always unpredictable because of the dislocations. These dangers, of tectonic or structural origin, can be classified according to the suddenness with which they occur, from brusque volcanic seismic eruptions to slow, sinister ground movements.

Volcanic eruptions cause relatively few deaths today because they can be anticipated. One of the great eruptions of modern times, the one of Mt. Bandai in the Tohoku area, is a good example. On July 15, 1888, a strong earthquake accompanied by dull rumbling preceded the actual eruption, which, in the course of some ten violent explosions, blew off the northern half of the summit. The ejected materials were scattered over 15 square miles, setting fire to several villages and killing 461 people. All the neighboring valleys were ravaged, and the topography suffered radical changes. The forested slopes on the northern side of the mountains became a barren desert, and the ejected material, blocking two valleys, formed a few new lakes.

Since World War II, Mt. Aso in Kyushu has erupted twice (April 1953 and July 1958), taking 18 lives. Myojinsho, on the Izu Islands south of Tokyo, killed 10 within one year (September 1952–53). But almost as serious as the deaths, which have now practically ceased, is the effect on the terrain, particularly on the intricate pattern of the rice paddies. From Daisetsu in Hokkaido to Sakurajima at the tip of Kyushu, there are active volcanoes everywhere, and to the inhabitants of the country they will never cease to be a handicap and a menace.

Seismic disturbances are serious because they are practically unpredictable, despite the patient research of Japanese scientists, and also because they can occur in any quarter of the land. Actually, they generally take place in certain areas; a study of the records reveals three particularly sensitive zones. One of these is the Boso Peninsula, less than 35 miles from Tokyo. The other two are on the Japan Sea, some 65 miles north of Osaka, and on the Pacific coast, in northern Tohoku and Hokkaido. Seismographs register about 5,000 shocks a year; however, not more than 30 are noticed. Every ten years, on the average, some part of the country is shaken by an earthquake that kills. In this regard, the greatest natural catastrophe in the history of the nation was the earthquake of September 1, 1923. All of Yokohama and most of Tokyo were devastated; 80,000 people perished and nearly 300,000 houses were destroyed, either by the shocks themselves that leveled the traditional wooden houses, built without foundations, or by the fires that followed. Even a slight tremor will shake the paper panels in a house out of their grooves, and should they fall into the hearth or some other unprotected source of heat, they will burst into flames that will quickly spread to the straw mats and the wooden walls, and shortly engulf the building itself.

Less dangerous, yet causing damage and considerable expense, are movements of the earth that, in certain areas, shake loose entire mountainsides. These landslides, generally composed of clay, may be from 20 to 75 feet deep, several hundred feet wide, and from 2 to 2.5 miles long. The speed of the flow varies with the season, from 6 to 23 feet a year, depending as it does on the water content of the soil. The land is capable of advancing almost one-half inch a day. Landslides are especially numerous in Hokuriku, on the Japan Sea side, where more than 10,000 have been counted and where they sometimes carry along with them an entire grove of trees, a paddy field, and even an occasional temporary structure. This makes it necessary for the communities affected to redistribute the land periodically because property at the tip of the flow steadily shrinks in size.

At the head of most of the bays where the great cities of Tokyo, Nagoya, and Osaka are situated, the land has been sinking slowly, causing buildings in Osaka, for example, to subside 1 to 1.5 inches a year, and as much as 4 inches in adjacent areas. Since 1935, the port area of Osaka has subsided almost ten feet. The reason for this is the constant pumping of potable water coupled with the drainage that is necessary before buildings of any size can be erected. This disturbs the physical balance of the soil, and a solution to the problem has yet to be found. The labor expended on maintaining roads and repairing broken water mains is a substantial item in the annual budgets of Japanese cities.

The Climate

The climate of Japan is no less responsible for the innumerable difficulties and dangers that its inhabitants must endure. The great variety of climates is surprising for so small a country, but Japan, of course, extends over several degrees of latitude, stretching from the shores of Soviet Primorsk to the tropical regions of Okinawa. Moreover, it is open to the south and the influence of the intertropical zone, and to the west where lies the vast continent of Asia with its winter weather. There are also great differences in altitude, sometimes within relatively short distances. In the archipelago proper the proximity or remoteness of the coastline, and the conditions prevailing in the west, on the Pacific, or in the mountainous zones of the interior contribute to this diversity and are responsible for the distinctive regional weather patterns.

MARINE AND CONTINENTAL

The climate is of two major types, marine and continental. In addition to the moderating thermal effect common to every body of water, the influence of the sea is felt here through the presence of the two great currents that bathe the shores of the archipelago. The more important of these is the Kuroshio, a warm-water current that originates in the waters between Taiwan and the Philippines. It divides and flows on both sides of Kyushu. The west branch follows the coast to the Soya Straits, opposite Sakhalin, where it delays the freezing of the Okhotsk Sea, which generally occurs only east of the Straits. The other branch washes the shores of southeast Kyushu and Shikoku and disappears north of Tokyo upon encountering the Oyashio, a cold-water current from the north that descends along the east coast of Hokkaido and Tohoku. The junction of the two currents causes plankton to proliferate; this in turn attracts large schools of fish.

The Asian continent is the dominating influence on Japanese climate, and the great thermal variations that occur on the mainland are the factor that in effect regulates the temperature and precipitation in Japan. In the cold season, Asia is the home of the Siberian anticyclone, while the Aleutian area is at the same time a zone of depression. Japan is situated exactly between these two centers of complementary action and consequently is swept by a north-to-south current of air that is cold and dry in the beginning but becomes variable and humid after passing over a few hundred miles of the relatively warm water of the Japan Sea. Other disturbances take place at the southern edge of this current, and these result in turbulence throughout the air mass. When the air current reaches the archipelago and the warm waters of the Kuroshio current, it becomes laden with humidity which it proceeds to discharge on the coast in the form of heavy snowfalls.

In the summer the situation is reversed. Asia becomes a low pressure area while the high subtropical pressures advance toward the Okhotsk Sea. The prevailing winds are from south to north; they move more slowly than the winter monsoons (three feet per second as against nine feet) and are much more irregular because of their saturation. From the high over the Okhotsk Sea the air moves southwest, forming a front upon contact with the tropical and equatorial maritime air that has come up from the south. The heavy rains of the hot season result from the passage over the archipelago of this front which follows the displacement of the high pressures over the Okhotsk Sea. The high pressures themselves follow the sun, and their passage to and fro is marked by two major periods of precipitation, one in June called the "plum rains" (*baiu*), the other, of lesser importance, in September. Between these two periods the archipelago is hot and humid and without rain. This cycle is excellent for rice culture, the first rains supplying the irrigation needed for replanting while the dry intermediate period hastens ripening.

From the end of summer and through October still more violent atmospheric disturbances occur. These are the typhoons. Their formation is greatly aided by the surface temperature of the sea, which at this season, three months after the maximum declination of the sun in the northern hemisphere, is at its peak. The air consequently is saturated, making it dynamically unstable and causing abrupt variations in pressure. The extremely warm waters of the Kuroshio may be partly responsible for the fact that the paths taken by both branches of this current are precisely those followed by most typhoons. Although the whole western region of the archipelago is affected, the Pacific coast up to the latitude of Tokyo suffers most from these devastating typhoons.

TEMPERATURE AND RAINFALL

The predominant influence of the continent is apparent from the temperature records. The seasonal temperatures in Japan are lower than those at similar latitudes on the mainland, due of course to the country's insularity. Especially in winter, temperatures are also several degrees lower than those in Europe because of the cold winds from the continent, humid on the west coast and dry on the east, that prevail for four months of the year. In many ways they resemble the temperatures on the east coast of the United States, since Japan, forming the eastern edge of a continent (the Euroasiatic continent), is exposed to the same general climatic influences. In Hokkaido, an absolute minimum of –40°C. (–40°F.)* was recorded at Asahikawa, which lies on a plain in the same latitude as Toulouse in southern France and Toronto in Canada. The rest of Hokkaido also has very severe winters: the annual average at Sapporo is only 6.8°C. (44.2°F.); Hakodate has –2.9°C. (26.8°F.) in January and 22.2°C. (72°F.) in July. The average in Tokyo in January is 2.4°C. (36.3°F.), and the most southerly regions can always count on several weeks of frost each year. In Shikoku and Kyushu particularly, summer is the dominant season because of its duration; but summer heat and humidity vary little from one end of the country to the other. The July average is 26°C. (78.8°F.) in Kagoshima and 22°C. (71.6°F.) in Sapporo.

As for rainfall, Japan has two well-watered zones. One lies between Kanazawa and Niigata on the Japan Sea coast. Here the winters are very humid because of the snow which blankets the villages and countryside for nearly four months. Takada, on the same parallel as Tokyo and situated on a plain near the sea, has almost 20 feet of snow each year. In the same period on the Pacific side, from Tohoku to Kyushu, the sky is clear, the air is brisk and stirred at times by icy gusts. Tokyo in January has one and a half times the sunshine of Rome, which in turn has more than Athens. In the summer it rains a great deal on both sides of the mountains, but on the Pacific slopes in particular, and nowhere more than between the Kii Peninsula and south Kyushu, where 104 inches

* The centigrade and Fahrenheit thermometer readings coincide at –40°C.

have been recorded, 64 inches in Kochi alone between May and September. Although it rains on this Pacific side only during the summer, the precipitation is greater here than on the opposite slope, where 93 inches fall between September and February. Between these two regions lie some relatively dry sectors where even droughts are not unknown. (There are barely 24 inches in the central basin of the Inland Sea.)

The cycle of seasons is thus quite distinct for each region. The main difference is the drop in temperature as one advances from the southwest to the northeast. This is best illustrated by observing an important date in Japanese life, the one on which the cherry trees bloom. When the first flowers appear in the gardens of Kyushu, about March 25, the Okhotsk Sea north of Hokkaido is still a frozen waste. About April 10 they bloom in the Kansai area and in south Hokuriku; about the 20th in Tokyo, the 30th in north Tohoku, and on May 10 in Hakodate, in southern Hokkaido. There are areas of Hokkaido that see no blossoms before May 30, by which time Kagoshima is beginning to feel the tropical heat. A similar schedule could be made for the number of days the country is free of ice. This amounts to 260 days on the westernmost tip of Kyushu, 240 along the Pacific shores from Nagoya to Tokyo, 200 at Sendai, 180 at the northern extremity of Honshu, 150 in central Hokkaido, and even fewer in other localities.

Thus, while the periods between seasons remain fairly constant, the summers and winters on the four islands vary in length. From four months each in the central region that includes Niigata, Tokyo, Nagoya, and Osaka, they last three (summer) and five (winter) months in Tohoku and Hokkaido and, conversely, five (summer) and three (winter) months in the subtropical regions of Shikoku and Kyushu. Nevertheless, the basic characteristics remain the same, at least those pertaining to summer: hot and humid everywhere and carrying as far north as Siberia the kind of tropical weather that exists for many months in the southwest. The two types of winter weather—dry and clear, mild and snowy—equally divide the archipelago longitudinally.

NATURAL DISASTERS

This type of climate is as responsible for natural disturbances as is the basic structure or topography of the country. The disturbances may be classified according to whether they occur with brutal suddenness or build up slowly and gradually. Of the former kind, typhoons are an outstanding example. From 1945 to 1961 they caused the deaths of 20,303 persons and destroyed 326,000 houses (an annual average of 1,500 victims and 20,000 buildings). Like earthquakes, typhoons destroy in two ways. First, they exert widely different degrees of pressure on buildings. Since many of these buildings lack foundations, they suddenly collapse. Then the winds spread fires that complete the destruction. Since early times, man has tried to protect himself against these dangers. In southern Shikoku, a particularly vulnerable area, houses are built behind a high wall that exposes only the roof. In other areas, as in Korea, the roof is protected by a network of ropes. Where tiles are used, they are held together by plaster that traces a geometric pattern on the sloping roof.

Typhoons are not the only ill winds that blow. In regions bordering the Japan Sea, the winter monsoon, laden with snow, is most feared. Therefore, on the Niigata plains, for example, the houses are surrounded by tall wooden fences on which large mats of rice straw are hung in the wintertime. In the neighborhood of Izumo, high well-trimmed hedges serve the same purpose. On the Kanto Plain, the wind is cold and dry but equally piercing; there, many houses are sheltered by a deep circle of trees.

Japan is possibly the only country in the world to suffer severely from both typhoons and snow. Along the entire Japan Sea coast, and especially in the Niigata–Kanazawa area of Hokuriku, snow covers the ground for almost four months, depositing a very thick blanket that is constantly renewed until March. The smaller streets of the cities are filled to the rooftops, leaving the houses dark and damp; since early times there have been arcades on the main avenues to shelter those who venture out. On certain railways, such as the heavily traveled Tokyo–Niigata line, usually a four-hour run by express, snow can block the trains for long hours at a time, and each year the cost of keeping open the lines of communication and repairing the damage to buildings is a heavy burden on the municipalities.

Certain regions, in particular northeast Tohoku and the Inland Sea area, occasionally suffer droughts, which damage the harvest one out of every ten years on the average. This happens when the weather front that is charged with the summer rains arrives over the archipelago too early and blocks the "plum rains."

But the real menace of wind and drought is the conflagrations they cause. Fires are one of the traditional calamities, and this country of wooden houses and open hearths appears to have done little to protect itself. Statistics show that fires are most frequent when the air is dry (in the winter, on the Pacific slope and in the interior), while the high winds of autumn and winter can turn small fires into major disasters. It is true that what little protection exists is well organized, but even if the average number of fires per capita is less than in the West, each fire causes far greater damage.

Still further damage can be attributed to the Japanese climate. Thermal variations, due to the annual variations in pressure at the active centers of the atmosphere, can be catastrophic. A drop of only two degress in the average for July can ruin the rice crop, particularly in the north where the growing period is brief. This period is shortest in eastern Hokkaido, where the summer fogs shut out the sun and prevent the rice from ripening. Even more serious, however, are the inundations so common throughout Japan.

The Waters

Although Japan is exceptionally well watered, the absence of large plains has precluded the formation of rivers of any size. The longest river, the Tone, which drains the Kanto Plain, extends barely 200 miles. Moreover, the mountainous character of the country and the absence of glaciers to regulate the flow of water cause the rivers to be highly irregular, depending as they do largely upon rainfall. The early summer "plum rains" can, in a matter of 48 hours, deposit from a fraction of an inch up to 20 inches of water that immediately flows into the river beds. These beds, depending upon the season, vary greatly. They can be wide stretches of gravel, often more than half a mile at the river mouth, furrowed by thin trickles of water in the winter, or they can become raging torrents, rushing to the sea in the season of the heavy rains. The peak period for water flow is from May to October, with regional variations due to typhoons that are most severe at the beginning of the autumn or to melting snows most frequent at the end of spring. The water courses are generally not navigable; they are frequently used for rafting logs, however, and serve especially to irrigate the rice fields which draw two-thirds of their water from this source.

On the other hand, supplies of water estimated to amount to many trillions of gallons lie underground. Artesian wells tap these sources in the metropolitan districts, furnishing some 45 percent of urban requirements, with 23 percent from natural springs and the rest from the rivers. The new industrial centers on the coast also draw heavily upon this source.

Lakes are another characteristic feature of the Japanese scene. They are of every description: of volcanic origin, or formed by dams, or nestling in fault basins; and they can be of every size. They decorate the landscape from Hokkaido to Kyushu and supply fresh water to the people living on their shores and to rice paddies. The biggest of these lakes is Biwa, 260 square miles in area, which fills a large fault basin east of Kyoto. This handsome body of water, the inspiration of poets since the Middle Ages, is threatened today not only by pollution, which has killed all life at the southern end of the lake, but also by the demands for fresh water from neighboring Osaka (connected to Biwa by the Yodo River, its outlet) and Kyoto (connected by a tunnel).

The hydrographic pattern is in itself one of the more spectacular sources of violence in Japan's natural environment. The rivers follow a steep gradient to the sea; where they cut across the plains, they flow between embankments that generations have imprudently raised to such heights that in places the roads and railroads must tunnel under them. Generally, however, these lines ascend very gradually to the bridges, thus permitting the rivers to flow at a level well above the surrounding plains. During the period of heavy rains great masses of alluvium, torn from the mountainsides, sometimes break through the embankments and cover the rice fields with a thick carpet of gravel and sand that is more devastating than the waters themselves. The spectacle of these angry waters forcing their way through some break in the embankment and inundating the adjacent fields is not uncommon. Each year, in many parts of the country, roads and railroads are torn up and swept away by the floods, and the neat mosaic of the paddies is covered by mounds of debris that must then be removed at great cost.

It is on the Pacific coastal plain, where the subsidence tends to keep the land continually submerged, that the greatest damage is observed. Nobi Plain, opening out on Nagoya Bay, is a prime example. It is slowly sinking into the sea and the movement is being hastened by excessive pumping in Nagoya City. The two rivers, the Nagara and the Kiso, that traverse the city carry a considerable volume of alluvial soil. Their multiple branches furrow the plain, forming a number of oblong islands that, for the past ten centuries, the inhabitants have surrounded with dikes to protect from the floods, thereby intensifying the danger. There have been rice fields here since the seventh century and the history of the area is filled with stories of man's struggle against this devastating element of nature. In the past century and a half alone, 110 floods have been recorded. Whenever a typhoon visits the area, adding torrents to the regular volume of water in the river, the whole plain becomes a vast lake where only the roofs of houses and people circulating between them in boats can be seen.

Soils and Vegetation

The interaction of structure and precipitation has given Japan certain characteristic soils over which has spread a rich and varied cover of vegetation. These soils are for the most part acidic since they are usually of volcanic origin, and they are poorly developed because of rapid erosion and tectonic activity. For this reason, zonal soils (which develop when climate and vegetation are stable) are scarce; podzol soils are more common and are gray in color in the north, red in the west. They cover the plains and terraces with a surface that discourages cultivation.

The intrazonal soils (due solely to the nature of the parent rocks and the drainage) are more numerous and generally volcanic. They are dark and acidic and in order to produce well must be treated chemically whenever found. On the Kanto and Nobi plains in particular they have collected in large areas and at different levels. However, it is the alluvial soils that are most widely distributed and that compose 80 percent of the total area. Some of these alluvial soils can be classified as lithosols; these are thin and coarse in quality and retain the properties of the parent rock. The other alluvial soils are more fertile, having begun to develop wherever found, and have been constantly improved by human effort. Whether sand or mud, their properties and location are the result of underground or surface drainage. They contain all that the Japanese paddy requires.

Most of these soils developed under a cover of vegetation. In fact, the forest at all times has been an outstanding feature of the Japanese landscape, and even now it covers 67 percent of the land surface, probably the highest percentage in the world for an industrial nation. That this has been possible in a country short of land is due to the fact that the forests are found in mountainous regions where the slopes are unsuited to rice culture. Wood, on the other hand, is an essential element of Japanese civilization: traditional civil and religious structures were, up until recently, constructed exclusively of it. And wood is also used to make charcoal, the traditional fuel of the country.

The forested areas show great variety because the archipelago extends over several degrees of latitude. In Hokkaido and the mountains of north Honshu, conifers mixed with birch, ash, and dense underbrush predominate. This typifies the eastern seaboard of any continent and is repeated across the water in Soviet Primorsk. Beginning in southern Hokkaido, but more particularly in central Honshu, conifers and broadleaf trees appear in equal numbers, the latter exclusively of the deciduous variety: oaks, beeches, and maples. And throughout the west, wherever the annual mean temperature is over 13°C. (55.4°F.), there are forests of the subtropical or "Chinese" type, characterized by tall conifers and especially broadleaf evergreens, camellias, magnolias, and green oaks; on the southwest coast are palm trees, camphors, and even a fruitless variety of banana tree.

These forests differ from other temperate-zone forests of the globe in the number of species they contain. This is because the great glacial periods of the Quaternary did not decimate all growing things that had survived the Pliocene period, as was the case in Europe. This variety still exists despite a great deal of cutting as well as intensive reforestation (1.25 to 1.5 million acres per year), leading to the replacement of broadleaf trees with conifers which have a greater yield capacity. Broadleaf trees still constitute about half the timber grown, but the number is slowly declining. Conifers furnish wood that can be used and pulp for making paper. Pulp used to be a specialty of Sakhalin, but since the loss of that island to the USSR, pulp is being supplied by Hokkaido. The great temples that were erected in almost every century from the time of the Middle Ages, the devastating fires that periodically ravaged the country, the growth of the big cities—all of these factors helped to deplete the forests, and the nation must now import lumber from countries of the northern hemisphere. Nevertheless, about ten percent of the forested areas, located near the mountaintops, still remains untouched, because these forests are difficult to exploit and are furthermore needed to regulate the water courses of the country.

Between 1,000 and 5,000 feet above sea level the forest sometimes gives way to an expanse of stunted bamboo, mixed with a coarse grass that grows like a shrub. This coarse grass probably replaces the ancient forests that were burned over. The bamboo characteristic of the Japanese countryside is found from one end of the archipelago to the other, growing in great clumps in the west and in thick groves of *sasa* in the center and north.

The Natural Regions

The many and diverse traits that terrain, climate, and

vegetation display throughout Japan are also found locally in naturally homogenous regions.

THE NORTHERN ZONE

The northern island of Hokkaido and the province of Tohoku, immediately to the south, constitute the first of these great natural regions. Winter, the long cold spells, the snow, and the short period of plant growth are its main features. Cut off from other regions of the archipelago and with a hinterland that is severely isolated, it contains in turn four distinct natural areas. Hokkaido is divided along a line extending from Cape Soya to Cape Erimo. The eastern half (I) includes the whole Daisetsu mountain range at the foot of which lie the cold, damp plains of Tokachi and Konsen. Fogbound in summer, arctic in winter, this is the most inhospitable section of the entire country. The western half (II), on the contrary, encloses extensive plains that are mild in summer and that, once drained, allow man to move about and plant. Mixed forests take the place of the conifers that are found only in the east.

Tohoku includes the Pacific slope and the central basins (III), a dry, bright region where broadleaf trees grow well on the flat, well-drained alluvial plains. The western side (IV) also has long winters, but they are snowbound, and the summers have a heavier rainfall. This is equally true of the northern sector of the Kanto Plain.

THE CENTRAL ZONE

The central zone corresponds to the widest part of the archipelago. It has at its center an axis (V) in which the tallest and most massive mountains in the country en-

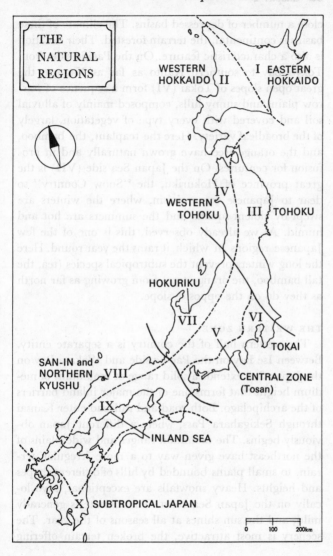

THE
NATURAL
REGIONS

I EASTERN HOKKAIDO

WESTERN HOKKAIDO II

IV WESTERN TOHOKU

III TOHOKU

HOKURIKU

VII

V

VI

TOKAI

SAN-IN and NORTHERN KYUSHU VIII

CENTRAL ZONE (Tosan)

IX

INLAND SEA

X SUBTROPICAL JAPAN

0   100   200km

close a number of depressed basins. The climate of these basins is continental, the terrain forested. Their isolation is also a characteristic feature. On the Pacific side, from Tokyo Bay to southern Kanto as far as Nagoya, the great open slopes of Tokai (VI) form a sequence of narrow plains and sunny hills, composed mainly of alluvial soil and covered with every type of vegetation, largely of the broadleaf variety. Here the teaplant, the bamboo, and the orange tree have grown naturally and in profusion for centuries. On the Japan Sea side (VII) is the great province of Hokuriku, the "Snow Country" so dear to Japanese romanticism, where the winters are swept by violent squalls and the summers are hot and humid. As we already observed, this is one of the few Japanese regions in which it rains the year round. Here the long winters prevent the subtropical species (tea, the tall bamboo, the orange tree) from growing as far north as they do on the opposite slope.

THE WESTERN ZONE

The western half of the country is a separate entity. Between Ise Bay on the Pacific side and Wakasa Bay on the Japan Sea extends a solid range of mountains of medium height that forms one of the major inland barriers of the archipelago. Both road and railroad enter Kansai through Sekigahara Pass, where a different Japan obviously begins. The mountain ranges and wide plains of the northeast have given way to a more irregular terrain, to small plains bounded by hills of different shapes and heights. Heavy snowfalls are exceptional, save locally on the Japan Sea coast. The climate is generally mild, and the sun shines at all seasons of the year. The scenery is most attractive, the broken terrain offering great variety and accommodating many types of settlements.

In this region, which includes Shikoku and Kyushu as well, there is still the double exposure to the Pacific Ocean and the Japan Sea. This is repeated in fact by the Inland Sea, situated at the center. On the Japan Sea side (VIII), small narrow plains lie at the foot of massive mountains, separated and isolated by steep escarpments which extend out to sea and form the numerous islands. But it is the climate that distinguishes this San-in region. The winters are humid, as they are all along this seacoast, even as far as Fukuoka in Kyushu, where snow is not unknown. Dense forests cover the heights from Mt. Tamba, north of Kyoto, almost to Hita, behind Kitakyushu.

In the heart of the west lies the Inland Sea, whose shores and islands form a world apart (IX); here the land is intimately joined to the sea, which stretches to the horizon. The climate is hot, and a luminous mist fills the air. But the region is especially dry, and olive groves flourish on Shodo Island. The heights to the north (Honshu) and south (Shikoku) form a double barrier that intercepts the winter monsoons as well as the rain-laden winds of summer. Lateral circulation is easy, for this is above all an "open region," a highway.

Finally, to the south and west lies subtropical Japan (X). It embraces the great valleys and southern shores of the Kii Peninsula in the Kansai area, south Shikoku, and Kyushu, almost to Nagasaki. Everywhere the narrow and heavily wooded plains that lie in the shadow of tall, massive mountains, volcanic in Kyushu (Aso, Kirishima), appear to be hemmed in by the terrain. The summers are long and wet, the winters brief and mild. Frequent and devastating typhoons are peculiar to the region and mark it as inhospitable. In the far south, the island of Kyushu literally crumbles into the sea, forming islands, bays, and a ria coast that offers doubtful shelter from the typhoons. As already noted, the vegetation is rich in tropical species, and from June to September the fine beaches of Miyazaki, where innumerable palm trees sway gracefully in the wind, pleasantly call to mind the shores of more southerly climes.

Of all these regions not one has been spared the more violent moods of nature. For this reason Japan must be considered an inhospitable land, hostile at times to human habitation. On a global scale, the subjection and occupation of the country must be considered one of man's most remarkable victories over nature. There is no calamity known to the world that the archipelago has not suffered; the many latitudes it covers lay it open to the excesses of the northern regions (cold, snow, frost, short growing period) as well as to those of the tropical zone (typhoons, torrential rains, intense heat, atmospheric humidity). Its youthful geological structure keeps it in a state of instability (earthquakes, volcanoes) that is a constant threat to man and his accomplishments.

Thus handicapped, the Japanese people have had to face the further danger of overpopulation. To feed, house, and clothe a constantly growing population under these conditions has been the challenge that man has had to meet here. If this challenge has been accepted—if beyond all expectation the gap between the basic instability of man's environment and the permanence of his institutions is slowly closing (and this well before the introduction of modern techniques for controlling that environment)—it is because he has developed a peculiar conception of his relations with nature that enables him to face it and either dominate it or endure its hostility. Moreover, Japanese society, essentially a group society and centripetal, from the beginning has had a unique structure that allowed it to take maximum advantage of individual effort by subjecting it ruthlessly to the collective will. It is now time to say who these people are, how they are distributed over the surface of their inhospitable land, and by what means they succeeded in becoming the masters of it.

+ **3**

The Japanese People:
Urban and Rural

The Occupation of the Islands

According to tradition, the Japanese people reached
the archipelago they presently occupy from the south,
after passing through Taiwan and the Ryukyus (an archipelago between Taiwan and Kyushu). More likely
some of the original groups came from the coastal regions
of present-day south China where they had been influenced by the peoples of southwest Asia; others came from
the continental regions of northeast Asia where they were
in contact with the Siberian races. These two distinct
branches had to reach the archipelago via the Straits
of Korea, only 100 miles wide; commingling on the islands, they formed the present Japanese people, a basically Mongoloid race. But when they arrived, they found
that other peoples had preceded them, among these the
ancestors of the Ainu. The invaders were in a more advanced state of civilization and gradually forced the other
tribes northward—not without some crossbreeding,
however.

The Ainu belong to a proto-Caucasoid, non-Mongoloid group that broke away so early from the other peoples of the white race that many of the physical characteristics we associate today with the latter never developed. Even today, however, the Ainu of northern Japan have relatively hirsute features, unusual among the peoples of the Far East.

Thus the Japanese, like all other peoples, are a complex mixutre of racial strains, and when seen in large numbers they present many different types. There is the slim, straight type, for example—fair-skinned, with a straight or slightly hooked nose and delicate joints. There is the short stocky type—rather dark-skinned, built with a small, and sometimes flattened nose. The Japanese differ from other Mongoloids, however, in their rather short legs; this gives their bodies a unique center of gravity, which differs from that of the Vietnamese or the Westerner (where it is at the base of the pubic area) in that it is situated halfway between the pubic area and the navel. The height of the Japanese relates him to the southern peoples of East Asia. The average height, in 1950, was 5′ 3″ for men and 4′ 11″ for women. Since then these figures have increased considerably because of the change in diet, in which animal proteins and fats now have a greater share. Thus between 1930 and 1970, the figures rose from 5′3″ to 5′5″ for male students and from 4′11″ to 5′1½″ for young girls. There are certain regional variations, but in general the height of the average Japanese increases as one moves from Kyushu in the southwest to the northeast part of the country.

ADVENT OF A RICE CULTURE

Japanese prehistory begins around the third millenium and is divided into two great periods, the Jomon (3,000

B.C. to 300 B.C.) and the Yayoi (300 B.C. to A.D. 300). This is followed by a protohistoric or Tumulus period which lasted to the sixth century, at which surprisingly late date the nation's actual history begins. This remarkably delayed development, which resulted in a serious lag behind the history of the Asian continent, was already evident in the Jomon period when China had husbandry and knew bronze (eighteenth century B.C.) and iron (fifth century B.C.), while Japan was still using stone artifacts and lived by hunting and fishing.

Yayoi culture brought an end to this primitive period. With the advent of rice culture the plains were systematically occupied, wooden farming implements fashioned, clay objects thrown on the wheel. The new culture first took hold in the west, while Jomon culture still lingered in the northeast. Bronze arrived from Korea in the first century A.D. and was used to make arms and ritual objects. Among the latter were mirrors of bronze and semiprecious stones carved in crescent shapes which the conquerors had brought with them. Since they could impose their ways upon the people of the land, they used these three objects as symbols of their authority; to this day the sword, the mirror, and the jade jewel form the regalia of the reigning family.

The historical sources are mere collections of myths, put into writing at a later time and difficult to interpret today. They state that three political centers existed in protohistoric Japan: one in northern Kyushu, cradle of the imperial dynasty; another at Izumo on the Japan Sea, where there still exists one of the most venerated of the national sanctuaries; the third in Yamato, north of Osaka. The third one gained the upper hand after struggle, compromise, and the arrival upon the scene of the imperial clan. It was from Yamato that the imperial clan set forth to conquer and assimilate other regions of the archipelago. The remains of the ancient capitals are still extant, notably the first one whose history is well known—Heijo-kyo, the Nara of today, erected in 710 in the style of the Chinese capitals of the period. In 794 the Court moved to another basin 30 miles to the north and built Heian-kyo, the Kyoto of today. There the capital was to remain for ten centuries, until the center of government was moved to Edo (Tokyo) upon the Meiji Restoration in 1868.

The country's western plains, therefore, were the first to be settled and introduced to rice culture. From there, military expeditions against the Ainu set out and conquered first the center of the island, then the north. Later great domains were established on which the warriors, their vassals, and their dependents settled, and gradually the civilization that was developing in the Yamato capitals spread throughout the land.

The Distribution of Population

Modern charts showing population density and the distribution of urban centers reflect in some measure this historical evolution. But the data are changing rapidly. This is because most of the population and national wealth is being concentrated in the long, narrow corridor that extends along the Pacific coast from Tokyo to the northeast of Nagoya, then again from Kyoto to Osaka and along the Inland Sea to the Straits of Shimonoseki and Fukuoka. This development appears irresistible and has been reinforced by changes in the economic activities of the population.

The percentage of the labor force employed in agriculture or fishing (the primary industry) dropped from 78 percent in 1872 to 51 percent in 1920; 39 percent in 1955; 34 percent in 1960; 24.2 percent in 1965; and 14 percent in 1975. Employment in Japan's secondary industry (mining and manufacturing) was 6 percent in 1880; 12 percent in 1900; 20 percent in 1930; 26 percent in 1940; 22 percent in 1950 (a decline probably due to agrarian reforms); 24 percent in 1955; 28 percent in 1960; 32 percent in 1965; and 34 percent in 1975. Tertiary industry (trade, transportation, and services) accounted for 12 percent of the population at the time of the Restoration in 1868; it had doubled by 1920, tripled by 1955, and reached 43.8 percent in 1965. It was 52 percent in 1975.

Since the end of World War II, this evolution has accelerated; for the ten years from 1952 to 1962, for example, the number of persons employed in agriculture fell 11 percent, while the labor force increased 38 percent.

Looking at the division of the work force in 1975 among primary, secondary, and tertiary industries (14, 34, and 52 percent, respectively), we can rather accurately situate Japan among the world's nations. It is similar to highly industrialized countries like the United States (4, 32, and 64 percent) and far from developing countries like India (72.9, 11.1, and 16 percent). However, within Japan these percentages vary considerably in different regions of the archipelago. To understand the variations, we must consider the density and urban distribution of the population in greater detail.

The average population density of Japan is 705 persons per square mile, a figure exceeded only by Belgium, Holland, and Java. In itself the figure has little meaning and hides some startling contrasts. To begin with, only the plains are actually occupied; when the total number of inhabitants is related to their surface area, the average rises to the remarkable figure of 4,922 per square mile. Moreover, the figure of 705 is the result of very diverse regional densities. These vary from 173 in Hokkaido to 1,857 in the Kanto Plain area. There is a clear difference between the northeast (Hokkaido 67, Tohoku 360) on the one hand and the center and west (Chubu 642, Chugoku 570, Shikoku 570, Kyushu 792) on the other. Like Kanto, Kansai, inhabited since ancient times and the site of the country's second conurbation, has the exceptionally high figure of 1,197.

Thus, with the exception of the Kanto and Kansai regions, all the larger sections of the country have population densities lower than the national average; Kyushu's figure is only slightly higher. A detailed analysis of the central Chubu region would reveal an exceptional concentration in the Tokai area on the Pacific coast, in Chugoku, along the Inland Sea, and again in the northeastern quarter of Kyushu. In northern Japan, in Tohoku, and particularly in Hokkaido, which was settled less than a century ago and has a short growing period (only one annual harvest is possible), the land is relatively uninhabited. In contrast, Kanto, Kansai, and the warm and humid west have been inhabited for centuries and are able to support large populations. Nevertheless, the use of the land simply for agricultural purposes does not explain these enormous discrepancies; urban distribution is the decisive factor.

Urban population figures have increased since the war and continue to rise faster than those for the population as a whole. The Japanese divide their country into vil-

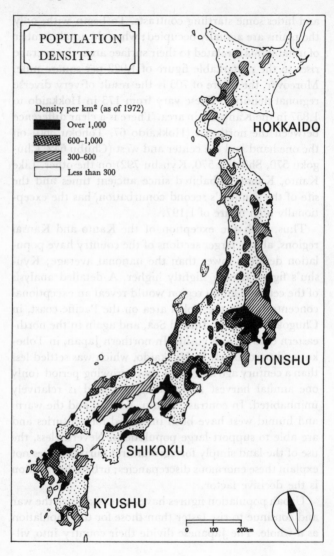

POPULATION
DENSITY

Density per km² (as of 1972)

■ Over 1,000

▨ 600–1,000

▧ 300–600

□ Less than 300

HOKKAIDO

HONSHU

SHIKOKU

KYUSHU

0   100   200km

lages (*mura*), towns (*cho*), and cities (*shi;* defined as an urban settlement containing more than 30,000 inhabitants). These are recognized administrative units, not just collections of habitations. Most cities include rather wide fringes of farms on their outskirts. Allowing for these, in 1960 the cities held 63.5 percent of the nation's total population. That same year, it was estimated that 43.7 percent of the Japanese lived in compact agglomerations of over 5,000 inhabitants. Today, the figure is over 50 percent.

This urban population is distributed very unevenly. Almost 60 percent reside within the six prefectures of Tokyo, Kanagawa (Yokohama), Aichi (Nagoya), Osaka, Kyoto, and Hyogo (Kobe); one-third live in the two prefectures of Tokyo and Osaka alone. Of the total populations of Tokyo and Osaka prefectures, almost all (95 percent in Tokyo, 84 percent in Osaka) are classified as urban residents. The figure drops to 16 percent on the Japan Sea coast (Tottori, Shimane); other prefectures where it is below 25 percent, with less than one-quarter of the population living in cities, are located in Tohoku, in the mountains of Kanto and Chugoku, and on the islands of Shikoku and Kyushu.

Birth Rates and Internal Migrations

The distribution of the Japanese population is the result of birth rates and internal migrations acting simultaneously. To understand the most recent population data, we must first look at much earlier birth rates along with those, for example, for 1960. In that year, the average birth rate was 17.2/1,000, varying from 20.9 in Aomori, northern Tohoku, to 14.9 in Kyoto and Kochi (Shikoku). Generally speaking, in the most distant sections of the country—in the north (Hokkaido, Tohoku, north Kanto) and in the southwest (Kyushu), which are rural and backward areas—the birth rates have remained above the national average. Figures below the average are found most often in southwest Honshu and in some sectors in northern Shikoku and northern Kyushu. As in most other countries, a low birth rate is also a characteristic of urban centers, but the large Japanese cities appear to have a slightly higher rate than is found in other industrial countries.

As for the mortality rate, there is less variation in the different regions, and the urban centers have the lowest (5.2/1,000 in Tokyo, 9.6/1,000 in southern Shikoku). Whenever the regional figures show an increase in population, it can generally be attributed to changes in the birth rate. These figures vary from 13.4/1,000 in Aomori to 5.3 in Kochi, and are even lower in the southwest (Kansai, Chugoku, and Shikoku). In the country as a whole, birth rates are higher in the villages than in the towns, and in the towns than in the cities.

On a map, the important areas of human industry and population show the country to be divided lengthwise into two zones. One zone includes the northern reaches of the country, all of the Japan Sea coast, and the southern islands of Shikoku and Kyushu. Here the population is young (over 30 percent are under 15) and workmen number less than 20 percent of the employed population, farm labor over 20 percent. Large cities are few, and, with the exception of Sapporo, all have less than 500,000 inhabitants. The second zone includes the Pacific littoral from north of Tokyo to Nagoya Bay, the Kansai plain, the Inland Sea borderlands, and northwest

Kyushu. Here are located all the metropolises, and here agricultural labor involves less than 20 percent of the working population; workers in secondary and tertiary industries make up one-third and one-half of it respectively.

The difference is due essentially to internal migrations, which tend to accentuate the contrast between the two zones. For one hundred years there has been an active movement of people from the rural areas that constitute the first zone to the second zone, with its metropolises and industrial regions situated on the Pacific coast and the Inland Sea. In the single year between October 1959 and September 1960, 7.4 million Japanese changed their residences, 2.5 million of them moving to another prefecture. As in most industrial countries, these migrations are of two, often complementary, kinds. The simplest and most frequent is the move to a nearby city within the prefecture; this can involve women as well as men and even entire families. The second means a definitive departure from the original home for one of the large industrial areas or one of the regional metropolises—Sapporo, Tokyo, Nagoya, Osaka, or Kitakyushu. In this case, the emigrants are generally young unmarried men who leave their home area because it can no longer support them. Most emigrants range in age from 15 to 30 years.

They settle in metropolises where a part of the population is not of local origin. Six percent of the inhabitants of Tokyo, 5.5 percent of those in Yokohama and Osaka, and 3.5 percent of those in Kobe were born outside these prefectures. In Tokyo, of the working population alone the figures are 8 percent for males and 9 percent for females.

Areas marked by departures or arrivals are easily noted. However, rather than simply classifying prefectures according to the predominance of "departures" and "arrivals," it would be more significant to point out those whose balance sheets (relation of arrivals to departures) show a change (even if negative), those in which the figures are stable (negative, neutral, or positive), and those which show a loss (that is to say, the prefectures where arrivals, even if more numerous than departures, appear to be declining). Among the areas belonging to the first category (those which actually attract or tend to attract more people than they lose) are the regions of Yokohama, Osaka, Kobe, and Nagoya (that is, all the large metropolises except Tokyo), and the prefectures adjacent to Tokyo, which year by year are recording fewer departures.

Regions in which the ratio of arrivals to departures remains constant are Hokkaido, which is probably reaching the saturation point, and Kyoto, lightly industrialized but lying within the Osaka residential orbit. Each year these two prefectures have an equal number of arrivals and departures. In this "stable" category can also be included the prefectures of Hokuriku (Niigata, Toyama, Kanazawa), those of the central mountain region (Gifu and Nagano), and Hiroshima, all of which lose the same number of inhabitants each year. The regions that are constantly in the minus column include Tokyo (where the balance sheet is positive but approaching zero because of the increasing attraction of the neighboring prefectures where life is healthier and the living cheaper) and, of course, all the lightly industrialized or nonindustrialized rural districts which for a long while have been supplying labor to the urban centers. In Tohoku, in towns on the Japan Sea coast (except Hokuriku), and in south Shikoku and Kyushu, the departures steadily outnumber the arrivals.

Among the factors influencing these displacements are the distances that have to be covered and the relative cost of urbanization. These play an important part, but even more significant, until recently, was the question of average annual income. If this differed substantially from area to area, the movements increased. Of late, however, this factor seems to have become less important. The wealthiest prefectures—that is to say, those that are most heavily industrialized—today actually receive a relatively limited number of immigrants compared with the adjacent zones, which are still largely rural and where the average per capita income is therefore more modest.

These internal migrations have also become more diffuse. They involve not only the largest metropolitan regions, but now the entire Tokyo–Fukuoka industrial belt is a target, as are the prefectures that lie between the big cities where new manufacturing centers have grown up on the coast. Among these are Shizuoka between Tokyo and Nagoya; Mie to the south of Nagoya; Okayama; Hiroshima; and Yamaguchi between Kobe and the Straits of Shimonoseki. Inversely, Fukuoka Prefecture, one of the four great "old" industrial regions, has been losing ground since World War II, and year after year the departures outnumber the arrivals. Finally, in the interior of this long, 600-odd-mile industrial belt, the movement has been complicated by lateral displacements from one city to another, or from old manufacturing centers to new ones that have sprung up in the areas between cities.

Types of Habitation—The House

The heart of a great Japanese city is certainly very different from the center of a humble village; yet from one end of the archipelago to the other, wherever man has chosen to build his home, the traditional house—with its brown wooden walls (plain or cement-covered) and gray-tiled roofs—displays remarkable uniformity.

This house is built entirely of wood. It has no foundation and is held to the ground by the weight of the heavy roof. It is quickly erected, following a standard design: a framework without angles, the walls of mud plastered over a bamboo frame or overlaid with plain boards. Most of these walls, sometimes well over half, are simple panels of translucent paper that slide on a double groove and that also serve as windows. When open or completely removed, they appear to increase the inside area of the house.

The houses are generally one-story, except in the cities, and are often surrounded by outhouses, the most prominent of which is the storehouse (*kura*) built of non-flammable materials such as plaster, brick, or cement blocks. It is used for storing the harvests and the family treasures, for the main house is often prey to flames. In the north and extreme west, the roofs are of thatch or reed, while in the cities and west (Kansai–Chugoku), they are generally of tile. Today, city ordinances forbid the use of thatch, and in towns as well as in the country colorful tile and sometimes brightly colored metal have become popular.

In its interior arrangement the Japanese house displays exceptional uniformity for a country of this size. The house plan, whether it be of a city or country house,

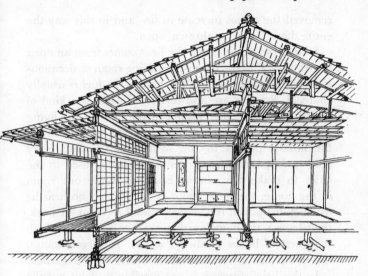

THE JAPANESE HOUSE

has three distinct floor areas: one section of beaten or paved earth that brings the outdoors into the home; another with a hard floor that is the area of communication and leads to the kitchen or to the "westernized" rooms; and finally the actual living section, its floor uniformly covered by thick mats of standard size (3' x 6'). These *tatami* are made of rice straw and covered with a fine rush mat. The floor in each room is spread with an even number of these mats, and the size of a room is always referred to by its number of tatami. The interior panels are wooden frames that slide in their grooves; they are covered with a heavy paper that shuts out the view but not the noise; the house, consequently, is far from soundproof. When the sliding panels are removed the rooms increase in size and in this way the entire house can be thrown open.

In the traditional home the heat comes from an open hearth built into the floor of the living room or occasionally in some other part of the house; the fuel is usually charcoal. Braziers are also used, and there is a kind of sunken fireplace called *kotatsu* in the floor of the living room, hidden by a table and a coverlet around which the family gathers in the wintertime. Today, every kind of gas, kerosene, or electric heater is used in the cities to make the winters bearable. Only one room in the house, the main room or *zashiki*, has no hearth; its chief distinction is a slightly raised recess at the back, the *tokonoma*, the home's esthetic center in front of which the guest of honor is always seated. In larger houses, this room has a verandah that opens onto a garden.

In this brief survey it is not possible to point out the diversity in regional architecture. It is actually as striking as in the older provinces of Europe; no traveler can fail to note the differences. The Tohoku region has large thatched cottages, the stable in a wing at right angles to the main building. On the Kanto Plain, at the foot of Mt. Fuji, are many two-storied houses with sunny attics for raising silkworms; the big farms in the central mountains are built like Alpine chalets but with roofs of board or bark. In Yamato (Kansai), the handsome country homes are uniformly constructed and have sleek thatched roofs. Kumamoto in Kyushu seems to favor multiple buildings. On the Japan Sea coast, almost all the houses of fishermen have board roofs that are weighted down with heavy stones; in Yamaguchi Prefecture, large structures with intricate interiors support impressive roofs of red tiles.

Farms and Villages—The Rural Community

The variety of sites selected for human habitation contributes to this diversity in the rural landscape. Whether clustered or dispersed, the houses are generally situated around the edge of the plains, aligned at the foot of the slope that marks the boundary to the plains, their backs to the mountain. Sometimes they form a straight line, straddling a road or some natural levee as in Hokuriku, or are grouped together in a square and surrounded by ditches, as in Yamato. Some may be perched at the very summit of hills or high terraces, overlooking the fields and terraced paddies. As in the uplands, they may be found clinging to ledges, halfway up the slopes that have been gouged out of the mountainsides. The latter are a common sight in the Totsugawa valley on the Kii Peninsula, in the heart of the mountains of Miyazaki in southeastern Kyushu, and in the wild hills of Kitakami in Tohoku, which the Japanese call their "Tibet." This same diversity is found among the villages of fishermen, some of whom build their houses on the beach or behind a line of dunes, others on rocks at the edge of the sea and even, as in Shikoku, on cliffs high above the sea. But most often they choose to build on shores that are battered by the monsoon gales that sweep across the Japan Sea or by the typhoons from the Pacific.

Besides the diversity in houses and their locations, the rural landscape itself offers variety; everywhere there are villages and hamlets in which men live in close association as well as isolated farms surrounded by fields or paddies. The dispersed rural habitation is common to all regions and is found on the plains as well as in the mountains: in the uplands of Shikoku, of Kyushu, more

frequently of Honshu (Chubu); in some of the Tohoku
basins (Yonezawa, Yokote); among the rice paddies on
reclaimed land in Ariake and Kojima bays and the
Hachirogata lagoon; and even on some of the oldest
inhabited plains like those of Tonami and Izumo on the
Japan Sea and Takamatsu in Shikoku. In Hokkaido, in
fact, this type of dispersion is found extensively.

On the whole, dispersion tends to become widespread
as the latitude and altitude increase, which in Japan
means later and more sparsely occupied settlements; but
some of the earliest inhabited areas also have this characteristic, in the west particularly. Whether these isolated
farms are situated on low or high ground, whether
surrounded by tall, trimmed hedges as in Izumo, hidden
in some grove of trees, or standing amid their paddies or
fields, they appear to follow no clear pattern of location.
Climate seems not to offer an explanation, since they
exist side by side with clustered dwellings and are just
as old. Their ubiquity might indicate that the current
belief in the connection between rice culture and the
group type of habitat (the latter an answer to the
problem of irrigation) in the case of Japan is not well
founded.

Any attempt to relate the number of dispersed
homesteads per region to population density, to the number of villages and their average size, or to individual
land holdings is futile. Equally futile is trying to relate
them to the time the land was first exploited. Whether the rice fields are old or of recent date, these isolated
farms have coexisted with the villages; in Hokkaido, for
example, where colonization has been well studied, the
two types of settlements were established at the same
time. Among the factors favoring dispersion are security

(the peaceful Tokugawa period encouraged it), fear of fires (which led big property owners to scatter the tenant farms), some natural obstacle to forming a community (for example, in Niigata, the presence of obstructive sand ridges on a plain subject to floods)—not to mention official regulations.

Japanese rural society is unusual because the social organizations of the "hamlets" and "villages" and their systems for exploiting the land do not depend upon the size of the community in order to function normally. They remain the same, however widely dispersed the inhabitants. If most farmers reside in compact clusters of houses—here as in all the Far East the lone rural habitat is the exception—and if these communities have a social structure that is highly cohesive, the same is true of the isolated farms which, by themselves or taken together, form administrative units which are also considered "hamlets" or "villages."

Whether he lives alone on his rice paddy or in the center of a big village, the Japanese farmer is aware that he is bound by a rigid and narrow system of rights and obligations with regard to his neighbors. First there are his family ties, hierarchical ties binding the senior branch to the junior and both branches to the tenants' families, even if the latter have become owners of their land. These family ties, of blood or adoption, are accompanied by obligations connected with the exploitation of the land which, in turn, take the form of associations of the most diverse kind: for the upkeep of roads and dikes; for the periodical repair of thatch roofs; for the exploitation of communal forests; and for community assistance at births, marriages, and especially at funerals, where each neighbor has his assigned task. Modern times have added to these obligations by creating cooperatives and associations for the loan of agricultural machinery.

Thus among the lonely farms on the slopes of Mt. Kitakami in Tohoku, of Kii in Kansai, or of Kyushu, as well as in the big villages of Yamato, the same spirit of solidarity unites the inhabitants. Whereas in France, for example, a village that still uses an ancient system of crop rotation and an independent farmstead in Normandy or Brittany would have two radically different types of land exploitation and social organization, the same is not true in Japan. Here, despite the variety of habitats, the house itself shapes the family life and thereby determines the social behavior of the individual.

The Cities

Every intermediate type, from the isolated farmstead to the compact village, is present, but, as Trewartha* has remarked, it is probably the semi-dispersed settlement, itself the manifestation of a complex and incomplete rural development, that is characteristic of the Japanese countryside. In contrast to this great diversity is the apparent uniformity of the urban community. From Fukuoka to Kyoto, from Kanazawa to Tokyo, to the northern cities of Sendai and Akita, everywhere the city presents the same appearance. Seen from the roof of a department store or a television tower, there are the same sea of gray-tile roofs feebly reflecting the sun, the same walls of brown boards, relieved here and there by the white plaster of a storehouse. A few trees and

* Glenn T. Trewartha, *Japan: A Physical, Cultural and Regional Geography* (Madison and Milwaukee: University of Wisconsin Press, 1965).

the great sweep of the temple roofs alone disturb the uniformity.

On the streets the houses are strictly aligned, the fronts differing little, the windows protected by thin wooden bars, the entrance sheltered by a tiled pent roof, a balcony on the second floor (the storeroom, if plastered), the roofs with prominent wide eaves. From the gate a narrow dirt passage leads to the rear, barely discernible in the semiobscurity. At the back (in the north country) or to one side (in the west), a single step gives access to the house. The rooms have mats on the floor and are separated by panels of translucent paper. Because the courtyards and buildings are generally long and narrow, they form a succession of house lots extending 70 to 100 feet back from the street, each one not over 16 to 20 feet wide. Sometimes a garden will have found room to grow in the middle of the narrow strip.

Japanese cities by their origin reveal the different stages in the history of urban settlement. Most of the large cities of today were once feudal towns, *joka-machi*, built around a castle whose walls and moats may still be extant (as in Tokyo, Nagoya, Osaka, Okayama, Hiroshima, Fukuoka, Sendai, Akita, Takamatsu, Kanazawa). Others were market towns that grew up where the plains and mountains meet, more particularly where the rivers emerge. Around the Kanto Plain, for instance, they form a regular ring. Some cities, *minato-machi*, were situated on the seacoast and served as ports (Niigata, Nagasaki). A third category, *monzen-machi*, grew up around great shrines like those of Izumo and Ise or the Buddhist temple of Zenkoji in front of which grew the city of Nagano. A fourth category of the traditional city is the post station, the *shukuba-machi*, strung along the highways of feudal Japan. When these roads declined in importance, many of the stations languished, although some, like Hamamatsu or Numazu, on the Tokaido highway, were able to participate in the economic life of the modern era.

Most of the cities of today originated in one of these four ways. Only Yokohama, Kobe, and the naval ports of Kure and Sasebo were founded in the industrial age prior to 1945. The cities of Hokkaido are barely a century old. Since the Second World War, however, the industrial and commercial growth of the country has led to the development of cities of a distinct type—agglomerations like Toyota, near Nagoya, built around a single factory (the Toyota automobile plant), or steel and petrochemical centers like Mizushima or Kashima, whose giant factories erected on reclaimed land have their commercial and administrative offices close by on the mainland.

Among the residents of a city neighborhood, as in the smallest hamlet, there has always existed a certain solidarity which in feudal times was imposed from above (the neighborhood association). Because the urban community has such recent and diverse origins, this spirit has not penetrated very deeply into the family tradition; nevertheless, it exists, and in the more popular quarters of the city the life of each family unit is quite closely associated with the life of the community. Various mutual-aid societies, cultural or social, and a natural inclination toward socializing (obvious in the summertime when people are tempted to live outdoors) tend to foster in each neighborhood a lively community spirit. In the new industrial cities, the sense of belonging to a great company inspires this sentiment.

It would be simple to classify Japanese cities according to their dominant or exclusive function—industrial, commercial, religious, shipping—but it is more significant to evaluate them for their importance to the life of the country by combining their functions and populations. Looked at in this way, they can be easily ranked. At the beginning of Meiji only 5 cities had more than 100,000 inhabitants. Today, 8 have more than 1 million (Tokyo, Yokohama, Nagoya, Kyoto, Osaka, Kobe, Kitakyushu, Sapporo) and 40 have over 250,000.

At the base is the category of cities of 25,000 to 100,000 inhabitants which provide a network of regional markets, of commercial, banking, and sometimes administrative centers throughout rural Japan. Those on the Pacific coast and the Inland Sea have become rapidly industrialized, while the others, in the interior or on the Japan Sea, still retain a strong traditional character. Next are the prefectural capitals whose activities derive from their administrative functions; these cities have from 100,000 to 400,000 inhabitants. Among them are the small regional capitals of Saga, Kagoshima, and Kumamoto (in Kyushu); Takamatsu and Matsuyama (in Shikoku); Kanazawa, Niigata, and Akita in the rural areas of the northwest; Kofu, Nagano, and Morioka in the interior; and Hakodate, Asahikawa, and Kushiro (in Hokkaido).

The present evolution of cities of over 500,000 inhabitants is quite characteristic. Along the country's industrial belt a string of agglomerations of over 1 million population is forming around the old cities of Sendai, Shizuoka, Hamamatsu–Toyohashi, Okayama, Hiroshima, and Sapporo in the northern reaches of the archipelago. These cities now serve as relay posts between the old metropolises (Tokyo–Yokohama, Nagoya, Kyoto–Osaka–Kobe, Kitakyushu–Fukuoka) and other urban centers; also, because they lie in the intervals between the big cities, they serve as centers of urbanization for the megalopolis. The latter is the major phenomenon in contemporary Japanese geography and will be considered in detail later. Let it suffice to say that Tokyo and Osaka are the two heads of the megalopolis and that the Shinkansen, the ultra-rapid railway line from Tokyo to Okayama, recently extended to Hiroshima and Fukuoka, forms the main axis.

4

The Elements of Control

EVEN THE most cursory survey of modern Japan will reveal a society marked by unusual numbers and an exceptional cohesion within the different social groups (family, business, etc.). It will also show certain intellectual values subscribed to by all and therefore very effective at every level of thought and action. This remarkable unity of mind and purpose seems to have welded 100 million Japanese into a body of unique strength.

To understand this unity is to understand how men have erected upon these rock-bound and unaccommodating islands one of the modern world's most formidable economic structures. In this chapter we will analyze Japan's techniques—material, social, managerial —and the intellectual values that govern their use.

The civilization itself grew out of an endless struggle with a natural environment whose hazards and inhospitable character have already been noted. This interaction of man and nature, for some 15 centuries, has led to the development of certain characteristic approaches to change.

An Uncontrollable Natural Environment

The Japanese environment is chiefly remarkable for its hostility to man. The constant spectacle of violence has given the people a special feeling for nature and has also shaped their views on what to do about nature. It has instilled in them a deep sense of the impermanence of things and has colored their attitude toward life in general. Buddhism, by stressing the transitory nature of men and things, has intellectualized what the environment had already shown to be true—that all human effort will perish and that the chain of cause and effect is in constant danger of being suddenly broken. Many of the national traits reveal the burden of this knowledge. A reluctance to define concepts clearly, which the vagueness of the language itself encourages, and a taste for the inductive method, since a logical solution may belie the facts—both are closely related to this basic attitude toward nature and man's place in nature.

Faced with such grave problems of the environment, another people would have developed a completely different attitude toward life or toward man's destiny. The United States is instructive in this regard. Its people, convinced that with the help of God they were masters of their fate, have treated nature with authority, clearing vast areas, destroying animal species, forcibly mastering the environment. Their present taste for the synthetic, the artificial, the conditioned "is but a corollary to the law that allows an entire continent to be remodeled," to quote J. Gottmann.*

* J. Gottmann, *Megalopolis* (New York: Twentieth Century Fund, 1961).

No attitude could be more contrary to the one held by the Japanese. Of course, the visible consequences to the landscape are similar in both cases: rivers harnessed, bays reclaimed, immense factories scattered throughout the country. Also similar are the economic and technical needs; but the mental attitude is completely different. The Japanese attitude was developed through a constant shuttling between the enjoyment of nature and the recognition of its intellectual and technical possibilities, between its demands and its gifts.

A Controllable Socioeconomic Environment

In contrast to the view of the physical world as uncontrollable, there exist in Japanese concepts of the social and economic world indications of exceptional control. Indicative of this control are the retention of a rigid hierarchical structure, the existence of strong economic directives, and a systematized approach to progress and change that is manifest today in the coexistence of values inherited from the past with techniques that are part of modern economic life.

Two distinctive forms of control operative in modern Japan were equally characteristic of the Japan of a thousand years ago. The feudal tradition and a tight family structure serve as bases of social organization.

THE FEUDAL TRADITION

The feudal tradition goes back to the old clans (*uji*) or great families in which the structure was strictly hierarchical, descending from the main family branch to junior branch to tenant, then to the artisans and serfs. The imperial clan in the beginning was simply the most powerful, assuming divine origin in order to perpetuate its preeminence. Japanese society never departed from this pattern: a few families to conquer the land, take possession of it, then exploit it. The great Taika (A.D. 646) and Taiho (A.D. 702) reforms tried to introduce the Chinese system of a central government directed by an aristocracy of letters recruited through examinations and also a system of land tenure based on periodic redistributions (the *jori* system). But both these reforms failed because of the tendency, at all levels of society, to base superiority on birth and family status. The system grew steadily more rigid within the feudal framework and reached its peak in the Tokugawa period, by which time the population was divided into four distinct classes: warriors, farmers, artisans, merchants. At the beginning of Meiji (1868), the feudal system crumbled, but the former samurai still held their dominant social position, even in the new world of banks, ships, and factories.

THE FAMILY TRADITION

The other pattern for Japanese society is the family, taken both as a collection of individuals strictly organized according to the Confucian code and as a distinct group somewhat aloof from the rest of society. As in China, the family forms the base of society, even though in modern Japan it has broken up and renounced its former primary function of acting as a unit of production and has become instead a consumer group. Blood relationship is not the only binding factor, as may be deduced from the way the system of adoption has persisted. It is the structure of the family, not the consanguine family, that is the model for Japanese society and that is used in all group formations.

Between the old unit of production that was the clan and the industrial or commercial company of today, the difference is only in generations. In rural areas we have seen that labor is the responsibility of certain groups, themselves hierarchical, in which family ties of blood or adoption reinforce other bonds of a strictly economic nature. In the cities, the family pattern again prevails, largely through the use of personal recommendations; after 1868 it was used to form the first industrial and commercial companies. The great prewar combines, the *zaibatsu*, were simply the most powerful of these organizations. In those days, having left their villages to seek work in the city, farmers were welcomed by these hierarchical establishments which alone were capable of helping them earn a living and which provided a social pattern similar to the one that existed in their native villages.

These ties of dependence are of a very personal nature. They are apparent wherever individuals are assembled and at every level. From the smallest shop where owner and workmen still refer to themselves as *oyabun/kobun* (parent/children), to the biggest companies where these relations still exist between the different ranks, the family pattern is very much alive. Its outward manifestation is an exaggerated paternalism which should not be judged by Western standards, for in Japan the "family spirit" existed long before any was created by economic factors. To this day, the workman or employee of a large company is retained until the end of his working days.

A COLLECTIVE MENTALITY

It is true that in every society there are reserved areas where, to all appearances, social controls are less strictly enforced. Religion and esthetic taste are examples in

Western urban society. It is also true that our most in-
timate aspirations are a reflection of the world we live
in, a world that forms and shapes our judgment. In
Western society, nevertheless, whatever the effect of
education or environment on our religious or esthetic
principles, it is always possible to modify or get rid of
these principles without sacrificing efficiency or one's
place in society. In Japan, on the contrary, these traditional values are part of the rules of collective living, and
to adopt them is not a way of escape from the skein of
obligations but rather a surrender to them and a tighten-
ing of their hold.

Let us take as an example the esthetic taste that plays
such an important part in every facet of Japanese life.
The appreciation of beauty is deeply felt and is based on
a special feeling for nature and on a universal appreciation of simple forms that remain close to nature. This
taste is expressed in terms that are difficult to translate
because they contain shades of meaning that are typically
Japanese. As in the West, a Japanese work of art offers
an insight into reality and is the source of certain specific
reactions.

But in Japan this esthetic judgment is rendered collectively. Japanese travel in numbers to admire the cherry blossoms or the colored maples of autumn; their
pilgrimages to the national sanctuaries are opportunities
for large groups to commune with nature. Even flower
arranging or the tea ceremony is enjoyed in company.
When an esthetic opinion is given it often turns into an
intellectual contest in which each one tries to find the
particular words which best express the group's feelings.
Thus, to love beauty is an act of allegiance to the civilization and therefore to the society. The traditional

Japanese house with its ancient architecture and materials that have been so carefully tended through the centuries is the perfect background for these esthetic values and for this love of beauty that has brought esthetics to the aid of social cohesion.

Application of the collective mentality to overpopulation results in an acceptance of conditions that would be considered adverse in a society less oriented to the group. The carefully adjusted wheels of society have had the effect, if not the intent, of making the individual submit completely to group restraints; in particular they have led him into respect for traditional values. This solidarity lightens his miseries and deceptions, as is evident in the group life of the hamlet or city neighborhood and even in the modern commercial enterprise where mutual aid is thoroughly organized. This solidarity also, to a certain extent, prevents the individual from becoming egocentric by making him share his joys, sorrows, and efforts with the group.

In addition, the Japanese have adopted an attitude toward poverty that has allowed them (and still allows them, to a certain degree) to live more comfortably in what would be considered uncomfortable circumstances. Their deep love of nature and the fatalism that is so much a part of their beliefs has led them to search for simplicity and austerity, perhaps in order to ward off a sense of misery. The stark features of the home and the simple daily fare reflect an esthetic of life that is the intellectual expression of poverty. Buddhism, it is well to remember, stressed the esthetic appreciation of poverty and called all its manifestations beautiful.

By getting the Japanese in their overpopulated country to recognize the importance of values held in common and adhered to collectively—values that excused the overcrowding—Japanese civilization was able to mold each individual and make his submission basic to his existence. The idealization of certain aspects of poverty, the acceptance of numbers as a help rather than a hindrance, a tolerance of others, and self-effacement—these, too, are some of the fundamental factors in the Japanese control of their social environment.

ECONOMIC CONTROLS

This wide acceptance of personal ties and dependence gives security and happiness to the individual but entails responsibilities at higher levels. Maintaining control of the environment means planning carefully, with the good of the nation in mind. For example, if a new petrochemicals complex, a blast furnace, a dock for ore ships, or a port to handle containers is to be built, detailed studies are first made to see how it will contribute to the development of the country at large and whether it fits the capabilities and the plans of the big companies.

Although the capital funds and most of the decisions or suggestions are furnished by the former zaibatsu, the state is gradually assuming an effective role. While it is true that the Liberal-Democratic Party presently in power strongly reflects the views of the business world, for a long time the government agencies, quite independently, have been giving their attention to these problems. Nature itself obliged them to do so, for the country is constantly threatened, and the government has had to take measures to anticipate natural disasters or to alleviate their devastating effects. Moreover, this willingness on the part of the authorities to control the economic and social life of the people rests on solid tradition.

This strict control of the economic life of the country is exercised in a typically Japanese manner. The responsible government agencies themselves are influenced by the close relations that exist among members of the government, the party, and the offices that grant the credits and authorizations. State control over private industry is effected in very special ways. The need to aid or eliminate marginal enterprises, to control investments, to raise the standard of living while stabilizing prices and salaries, to industrialize the country intelligently on a regional basis—all of these matters require frequent intervention by the authorities.

These actions are directed by the Ministry of International Trade and Industry (MITI), which exercises indirect but strong pressure, granting or denying requests for licenses or investment permits. However, the existence of relations based on obligation between government employees and private industry (extreme politeness is an expression of this) serves to ease these contacts. Of course, the eminently personal nature of these relationships can lead to inefficiency or delays. For one thing, the notion of public service suffers, and this helps to explain the country's paucity of sewage systems, libraries, and housing. On the other hand, the friction and maladjustments common to any large-scale planning are minimized and, on the whole, the Japanese economy in its own way manages to function smoothly under government supervision.

These personal relationships pervasive in the economic environment presuppose an understanding of why they are necessary and how they are to be used. Japanese education takes care of this from early childhood by instilling the rules in each child in the Confucian manner, through example rather than precept. Relatively free till the age of seven or eight, the Japanese child is then slowly but irresistibly drawn into the complex of duties and obligations and quickly acquires a clear understanding of his place in the group hierarchy. As an adult, he is supposed to apply the rules that govern his conduct to every act in his private and business life, largely at the expense of his emotional life. Should he fail to do so, his personal and public life will suffer.

To the foreign observer, the most remarkable manifestation of this control is unity. The overwhelming impression is one of a nation whose people are closely united, sharing the same ideas and having a common standard of behavior.

The Japanese themselves are well aware of their native qualities. Few people in the world are as cognizant of their peculiar traits—which they sometimes exaggerate. The number of books that appear each year on "Japan" or "What It Means to Be Japanese" is evidence of the intense desire to preserve this originality and this civilization that has shaped ways of thought and action and that provides a pattern outside of which life seems impossible.

In this sense, the word "Japan" represents something much stronger than "The United States" or "France," and the Second World War revealed what this was to the world. The possession of common ideals, emanating from a strong national tradition and a social structure acceptable to all, enabled the country to progress industrially and militarily in a manner that far exceeded its real power. These same qualities exist today, at the service of an economic expansion that is pacific but voracious.

Since World War II, Japan's relations with the outside world have been on a new basis. Although forcibly deprived of its former possessions, Japan is still vitally interested in establishing an economic foothold abroad, but its commercial and political negotiations are conducted with characteristic reserve. It does not try to export a culture it recognizes as being different, nor does it try to establish itself permanently or firmly in any country; in the case of the underdeveloped nations, Japan even hesitates to extend aid that is too substantial. It is enough, Japan finds, to have commercial missions, factories, business connections, and just a few indispensable men stationed abroad. The latter always consider themselves temporarily "detached" from society at home, and when their mission is completed they hurry back to their islands.

For it is only at home, on his familiar round of duties and obligations, that the Japanese feels that he is completely himself. His innate suspicion of the non-Japanese world and his attitude toward the foreigner, "the man from outside," come from a feeling of insecurity. They reveal a need to be assured that he is an integral member of a society that is his own and whose rules he observes exclusively, since only these rules give his life meaning and satisfaction.

This attitude explains many of the hesitations and advances that surprise the Western businessman. There have to be many meetings before a Japanese can appraise his foreign associate and commit himself in his dealings with him. Similarly, when he himself goes abroad his approach is cautious, however attractive the proposition. The slow pace of the continuing Soviet-Japanese talks on the development of Siberian resources, for example, is due largely to such delays, to the Japanese fear of saying or doing more than is required—in short, to a vague but deep suspicion of the world outside which is characteristic of the Japanese people at large despite their apparent eagerness to set out and conquer it.

Selective Assimilation

That vague but deep suspicion of the world outside has historical roots in Japan's cautious, highly structured approach to the assimilation of alien cultural patterns and techniques.

For twelve hundred years successive introductions of ideas and procedures from China alternated with long intermediate periods of readjustment. The discovery in the sixth and seventh centuries of Chinese culture—in particular of Buddhism, ideograms, and new ways to govern—was followed by fresh philosophical concepts, art forms, and techniques from the same source in the Heian, Kamakura, and Muromachi periods.

The assimilation, however, was selective; whatever appeared to be incompatible with the existing social structure was rejected (for example, centralized government in the Middle Ages), while the rest was accepted but remodeled to suit national "tribalism," as H. Nakamura* has pointed out in connection with Buddhism. This process was repeated for Confucianism and all the other ideologies that were welcomed later, often with enthusiasm.

The new techniques were added very deliberately to the ones already in use. Nothing was upset; changes were made gradually so as not to disturb the established equilibrium. This way of doing things seems to derive

* H. Nakamura, *The Ways of Thinking of Eastern Peoples* (Tokyo: Unesco, 1960).

from two constants in the Japanese mentality. On the one hand, as we have already said, the Japanese have no faith in abstract reasoning that experience cannot immediately justify. To introduce a new element into a given system—whether practical, such as the construction of a house, or intellectual, like the attitude toward nature—is to endanger a stability attained through centuries of practice. Anything added or suppressed must therefore be temporary and may be discarded unless it turns out to be a total success.

More generally, the innovation is a strain on the established order which in itself has a positive moral value. Every invention is automatically considered dangerous simply because it violates tradition. Inversely, to obey a master who speaks for the past or to imitate the works and thoughts of a prominent representative of orthodoxy are worthy acts because they help to maintain tradition. By faithfully expressing ideas and behaving in ways consistent with the country's culture, one helps to perpetuate those ideas and customs, and the strength of the system is simply the sum total of these innumerable individual acts of loyalty.

It is from this point of view that one must understand and judge both the Japanese tendency to imitate and, in a larger context, the static nature of Asian societies, which is merely their way of refusing to be destroyed. Among the factors contributing to the static society—or in the extreme, to stagnation—the desire to preserve a social structure considered indispensable to the survival of the group is the most important.

In this connection, the Tokugawa period offers an example that is probably unique. For two and a half centuries an authoritarian government systematically closed all the doors to the country and pressed its people into a rigid mold in order to form a definitive social structure. The effort to standardize the home is merely one instance. Consequently, when Japan was opened to the West, the country disposed of a number of techniques governing the practical aspects of life (production, transportation, exchange), society (a feudal system), and the spirit (neo-Confucianism, national Shinto). All these were little changed from what they had been in the sixteenth century, and effected a way of life that had disappeared in the West with the Renaissance.

However, even in the spectacular progress of the Japanese since that time (1868), during which they adopted, often with exaggerated enthusiasm, Western ideas and methods of production, certain conservative tendencies were apparent that are yet visible in the contemporary economic and social picture. To the Meiji leaders, with the destiny of the country in their hands, it was less a question of making the country into something resembling a Western nation than one of borrowing from the West whatever was needed to survive and to preserve Japan's precious traditions.

It was in this spirit that the Japanese slowly assimilated their borrowings from the Chinese and, similarly, copied Western techniques, once satisfied that their use would in no way endanger Japan's own traditions or its political independence at a time when the West was carving out vast colonial empires in Asia. Moreover, for a people pressed by numbers and time, foreign inventions represented, and still represent, a real source of streamlining. Largely because Japan decided to borrow these techniques rather than try to discover them for itself, it was able to acquire economic power very rapidly.

The last wave of foreign influence, coming from the West, probably caused no greater shock than did the first from the neighboring Asian continent, 14 centuries earlier. Spectacular as they were, these successive contributions, including the last, have merely made it all the more difficult to discern the immemorial traits, pre-Chinese, that still exist in today's society.

EAST-WEST CONTRASTS

The West likes to contrast the Japan of great cities, exaggerated Americanism, air travel and fast trains, air-conditioned offices, Western food, and art forms reflecting Western sensibilities, with the "traditional" Japan in which daily life is spent on the straw mats of the home, in which native food, clothes, amusements, arts, and folk crafts exist alongside the other and perpetuate a mode of life that belongs to another age. We forget that the same people who travel on trains at 120 miles an hour, sit comfortably in chairs, wear clothes fashioned by the best of tailors, and construct dams and factories as modern as any in the West, can remain stubbornly faithful, despite an occasional compromise, to the customs of their forefathers when it comes to food or lodging or a taste for literature and art. These contrasts, which are so obvious to Westerners, Japanese themselves notice only after making a mental effort. Adopting Western customs and techniques has in no way affected their own mode of life or work, and innovation, whether of Chinese or later Western origin, bears the unmistakable mark of their own civilization. Without that mark, it could not have been assimilated.

The most revolutionary ways of life and thought when borrowed from the West are themselves given a distinct

Japanese coloration as soon as they reach the archipelago.

Examples are not hard to find among the techniques themselves and in the attitudes that govern their use. It is interesting to see how the most modern methods have been introduced into certain strictly traditional activities and, inversely, to see the continued use of old techniques in establishments of major importance to the national economy. Everywhere, in certain quarters of the cities as well as in the country, craftsmen can still be found exercising their skills as in days gone by. Entire villages or neighborhoods are occupied by papermakers, potters, weavers, and carpenters, turning out work for which there is a steady demand. While industries boom, domestic life has evolved very slowly in certain respects, and a wide variety of traditional objects—household mats, paper panels, ceramic wares, certain kinds of fabrics— are still in daily use. The tools used in their manufacture are peculiar to the Japanese, and the way they are handled implies a special kind of training. (The saw and the plane, for example, are drawn toward instead of away from the body as in the West.) These crafts persist despite the use, by this same society, of modern tools.

We can note a dual tendency. On the one hand, the machines that require a highly specialized work force are being gradually automated because Japan lacks this very type of skilled labor. Steel mills and assembly plants are being operated by small numbers of workmen, and this speaks well for Japanese labor and its technical efficiency. The other tendency is seen in the great numbers of workers on one of the many construction jobs found throughout the megalopolis, or in the department stores and the public services. Here we see the problem of supporting an excessive supply of nonspecialized or quasi-specialized labor that must at any cost be assured of a living.

A third category of tools, most of them quite old and out of date, lies midway between the traditional ones mentioned above and the modern machine tool. These have survived alongside the craftsman and the factory because of the number of workshops, family owned and managed, that provide a livelihood for the people dependent upon them. There coexist, therefore, these three methods of manufacture corresponding to the three stages of technical evolution: the handicraft stage, the small-factory stage of the 1890–1930 period, and the present stage of the great combines, largely automated. Each stage corresponds to a certain state of society and to its specific needs, and gives the farmer, the artisan, and the industrial worker proper control of his environment.

This specific Japanese way of acting upon the environment is a very careful blend of the old and the new because of the need to introduce innovations gradually in order not to disturb the social balance. Allowing the past to survive while profiting from some innovation results in the innovation preserving a state of things it was meant to destroy. Tradition immediately puts its stamp upon the present; in no other country does the modern help in this fashion to perpetuate a way of life or a method of production that belongs to the past. Yet the prodigious success of the economic life of the Japanese of today is ample proof that nothing archaic is checking this progress. On the contrary, this blend may even be the Japanese key to that progress.

On the other hand, the very strength of this Japanese impetus suggests the possibility of an unlimited progress that some day will forget this concern for the past. The

Japanese economy gives the impression of great momentum, controlled with difficulty and constantly in danger of "overheating." It is clear that the original objectives have been attained. Overpopulation is no longer considered catastrophic; mastery of technique has resulted in more land under cultivation and control of the birth rate; there is diversity in food production; vast industrial areas have been developed; and the standard of living has been raised for all classes of society. There is the danger, of course, that the advance will overshoot the goals; although undertaken in the name of preserving a tradition thought to be indispensable, it could lead the country into paths that are alien to that tradition.

This current impetus is characteristic of the present Japanese control of the environment and contains elements that are easily analyzed: a rare gift for imitating foreign techniques; a need for quick returns (for there is never enough time and, anyway, one cannot depend upon time); a certain audacity in connection with investments and returns (on a scale seldom seen before in the world); and a self-confidence that has been justified by the results. Also noticeable is a sense of superiority, very personal and difficult to hide the more apparent the success, which is in part responsible for a latent xenophobia and which feeds upon its own triumphs. Nevertheless, the strength of this Japanese impetus comes mainly from the same source as its love of tradition: the stubborn intention to keep alive the values and a social structure inherited from the past.

A Dualistic Character

In summary, looking at Japanese society today, one

must conclude that the psychological and social forces behind the prodigious effort to transform the country materially are actually no different, in principle or application, from those used in the administration of these islands since the dawn of Japanese history. The two faces they seem to present today, the "traditional" and the "modern," are both necessary to the nation's survival in the modern world.

Only the first one allows the individual to share in the common task of developing the environment. For he is incapable of standing apart, even in thought, from the group society formed by his civilization or, for example, of responding to the class consciousness of the Marxist, since this presupposes a loosening of the hierarchical ties in order to join freely with other individuals considered his equals. Since he has above all a deep feeling of dependence upon others which severely restricts his individuality, he finds it almost impossible to think of himself as outside the web of obligations that his family and his daily life have woven about him since birth. Even the organizations that might have helped him to break away, the Communist Party, for example, or the reform movements, soon bear his mark. Factionalism, which often disrupts the concerted action of these basically revolutionary organizations, is the result of a desperate need to recreate some sort of small and distinct social group, and seriously limits their effectiveness, at least for the time being.

It is inside the traditional social group that the Japanese learns and adopts the modern ways of managing his environment. These ways, in Japan as elsewhere, are expressed in terms of power plants and capital, in production figures, in profits and investments, and in human beings who produce and must be fed. These ways, more-over, lose none of their efficiency by being adapted to Japanese society. They are protected by social and moral standards that recognize the hierarchy, leaving the field open to the few who show initiative and assuring them of the respect and submission of the masses. These masses also form themselves into groups in which the individual effort is submerged. The acknowledgment of reciprocal rights and, more particularly, of duties, discourages self-assertion and greatly reduces the friction that is inevitable in an age of industrialization. Even though in Japan today, as in the West, power grows out of an infinite sum of human miseries and servitudes, even though strikes of a violent nature sometimes occur, it is nevertheless almost inconceivable that a great revival movement such as socialism could take root here.

Both modernization and loyalty to tradition, therefore, still appear to be necessary in order to maintain the control Japanese society exercises over its geographical surroundings. The "Americanism" and the "archaism" that Japanese society is accused of are merely obvious aspects of this dualism. This dualism will continue to be a major characteristic for a very long time, for it reappears in all areas of human activity—in agriculture to begin with, where so much of the past still lingers.

Man and the Soil: Food for the Millions

THE CONCENTRATED and organized effort the Japanese devote to their natural environment varies by region. Throughout the land, modern industrial and urban centers with their vast residential and manufacturing complexes offer a striking contrast to the open country that presents, as it has for centuries, a flat expanse of paddies that change only in color with the seasons. However, even in this seemingly unchanging countryside there are sharp differences; next to the patchwork of fields, dikes, and canals dotted with small villages stretch new areas, recently drained or cleared, where orchards, silos, vinyl hothouses, and cattle barns give evidence of modern methods of agriculture. Of course, the countryside evolves slowly because it must follow a natural rhythm, but the manner in which man divides and works the land today is rapidly being transformed as the demand grows for more butter, milk, meat, eggs, fruit, and vegetables.

The Products of the Soil

Agriculture must therefore pursue two different courses. The main one is still the cultivation of the traditional

107

plants that are at the basis of the national diet. This, of course, means rice. Rice production keeps increasing steadily and fluctuates between 12 and 13 million tons, according to the year. It preempts about three-fifths of the 12.5 million acres under cultivation, which clearly places Japan among the major rice-producing countries of the Far East. As in northeastern China, rice grows here in the most northern latitudes, and at one time even reached the frozen shores of the Ohkotsk Sea. The yield is the highest in eastern Asia: from an average of 1.84 tons per acre it rises to 2 and even 2.4 tons on the Tohoku and central Honshu plains, dropping to 1.2 tons in the mountainous prefectures of the southwest where it must be planted on terraced slopes. Wheat (0.2 million tons on 210,000 acres in 1975 as against 1.29 million tons in 1965), barley (0.17 million tons as against 0.72 million tons), and other grains are rapidly decreasing in yields.

Still cultivated in the traditional manner are a variety of peas and beans which the Japanese consume in greater quantity than any other people in the world (1.4 ounces per day per person), turnips (3 million tons per year), cabbages (1.5 million tons), and cucumbers (0.9 million tons). Sweet potatoes, like rice, belong to the stock of edible plants of the tropical zone; various kinds are cultivated in the southwest only; in 1973, 1.5 million tons were produced. Further development, however, has been checked by the recent introduction of the potato (3.5 million tons). Other examples of traditional agriculture are the teaplant, which produces 95,000 tons on 135,000 acres, and the mulberry tree, which is grown extensively (10,000 acres) in southern Kanto.

Growing beside these traditional plants are some that are more familiar to the West. Orchards have spread over extensive areas of northern Honshu and the central basins; apple trees produce 1.2 million tons of apples each year, while the mandarin oranges on the slopes of the Tokai mountains around Shizuoka in Tokai supply 1.6 million tons. In the category of "exotic" plants found on the northern island of Hokkaido are the potato, tobacco, and the sugar beet, which supplied about 460,000 tons of sugar in 1975. Finally, in this country where only the horse used to be bred, barnyard animals are now being raised on plateaus, cleared slopes, or on the large farms of Hokkaido and Tohoku. In 1976, 1.8 million dairy cows, about the same number of beef steers, 7.5 million hogs, and 240 million chickens were being raised. The number of horses has dropped to 36,000 (from 1.4 million in 1935), of which three-fifths are in Hokkaido.

Taking the production index for 1961 at 100, an increase over the period of 15 years (until 1976) appears only for vegetables, 145, and fruits, 225. Animal husbandry registered a most spectacular advance, especially hogs, 330, poultry, 300, and dairy cows, 280. These basic food products have shown an improvement in quality as well as quantity. The land is being worked today by only one out of every four to five inhabitants, not always full time, and the product of their labor represents only one-tenth of the gross national product; nevertheless, it manages to feed about 60 percent of the 100 million Japanese, a remarkable proportion for a great industrial country.

Traditional Agricultural Practices—Fields and Rice Paddies

Modern ways of working the land are seen only in certain areas; everywhere, the rice field occupies most of the countryside, and its lack of a standard size or shape helps lend variety to the landscape. The extraordinary ubiquity of the paddy betrays a hunger for land that has possessed the Japanese farmer throughout the centuries. First he occupied the alluvial plains which had to be laboriously drained and irrigated; next, he settled on the lower terraces, watered by wells and ponds. He then climbed the slopes, even the steepest of which he carved into wide steps. Swamp lands and coastal bays like Kojima and Ariake were conquered next. Finally braving the northern latitudes, the farmer reached the shores of the Okhotsk Sea.

The varied aspects of the rice fields are due also to the unequal length of time they are given to mature (from eight months in the southwest to only four in northern Hokkaido); brown as the earth in winter and spring, in June the fields turn a pale green that becomes lightly golden in summer and finally a colorless stubble when the autumn harvest is done. On the Japan Sea side they are buried under a dazzling carpet of snow from November to March. In other regions, some other plant, wheat perhaps, will take the place of rice in the winter, and in certain very limited areas of Shikoku and Kyushu a second rice crop is sometimes harvested.

The landscape of rice fields is strikingly empty. Only a network of little dikes and canals, with a few ponds here and there, breaks the monotony. There are never any fences, but in some places in the north and northwest the fields are dotted with posts on which the harvest is piled to dry. The fields are often extremely irregular in shape as a result of centuries of subdividing the family property. Occasionally, where they could be properly

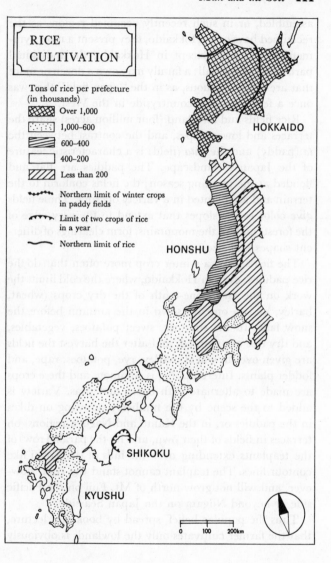

RICE
CULTIVATION

Tons of rice per prefecture
(in thousands)

- Over 1,000
- 1,000–600
- 600–400
- 400–200
- Less than 200

〜〜〜 Northern limit of winter crops
in paddy fields

〰〰〰 Limit of two crops of rice
in a year

—— Northern limit of rice

HOKKAIDO

HONSHU

SHIKOKU

KYUSHU

0   100   200km

assembled, or in such recently occupied regions as the reclaimed bays or in Hokkaido, they present a more symmetrical pattern. Except in Hokkaido, the individual parcels are very small; a family may own a dozen or more that are not contiguous, as in the "open field" that was once a feature of the countryside in the West.

Rice fields and farmland (four million acres) share the terraces and lower slopes, and the contrast between the *ta* (paddy) and the *hata* (field) is a characteristic feature of the Japanese landscape. The paddies are flat and flooded at the planting season; the fields conform to the terrain and are planted in a variety of crops. These fields give color to the slopes that extend to the very edge of the forests and, in the mountains, form clearings of different shapes and sizes.

The fields grow a winter crop more often than do the rice paddies; even in Hokkaido, where the cold limits the work on the farm, one-tenth of the dry crops (wheat, barley, and so on) are sown in the autumn before the snow falls. In the summer, sweet potatoes, vegetables, and dry rice are planted, and after the harvest the fields are given over to wheat, barley, rye, potatoes, rape, and fodder plants. Intercropping is common, and these crops are made to alternate with beans and peas. Variety is added to the scene by the mulberry, growing on dikes in the paddies or, in the Kanto and Nagoya regions, on terraces in fields of their own, and by the parallel rows of the teaplants extending over the hills of the Tokai like contour lines. The teaplant cannot stand the cold, however, and will not grow north of Mt. Fuji on the Pacific side or beyond Niigata on the Japan Sea side.

Thus the popular belief, spread by book and lecture, that the farmer cultivates only the lowlands is obviously false. Three quarters of a million acres of rice fields and 1.5 million acres of farmland are found on slopes of over 15 degrees; in the central basin of Honshu, in Hokuriku, near the Inland Sea, and in Kyushu, paddies are found on even steeper mountain slopes. In June, the little flooded fields share the summits with the conifers and the sides of the valleys are covered with their terraces, a small reservoir at the top supplying by gravity the water needed for irrigation. These terraces are no longer being built, but the mountains are still being invaded. Pasture lands, orchards, and vineyards are climbing new slopes everyday, pushing back the forest and the wide fields of scrub bamboo.

The widespread growing of winter crops has increased the production figures of the acreage actually planted. It is estimated that 133 percent of the arable soil of Japan is cultivated; in other words, that it grows 1.33 crops per year. The percentage varies in each region according to the length of the growing season. In the subtropical regions of the southwest that are hot and humid it reaches 180 percent, while in the cold, damp areas of Honshu it is only 101 percent, or an average of one crop a year. In Hokkaido this figure drops to 98 percent, and in some places to 85 percent due to an early or a late frost that damages the crop every three, four, or five years.

Paradoxically, in this country of rains it is drought that in certain parts of the land causes the greatest damage. For this reason the spread of rice culture had to be accompanied by irrigation. Ninety-five percent of the rice fields are flooded at the time of planting; 75 percent of this water comes from rivers and lakes, 8 percent from springs or underground sources, and 17 percent from rain catchments. The latter are especially numerous in the Kansai and Inland Sea regions, which are densely populated and suffer regularly from droughts. In the eighteenth century, a network of canals, fed by watercourses, was constructed by certain progressive daimyo whose income in rice depended upon these facilities. Great reservoirs were built after World War I, and the water was pumped out by hydroelectric power for the use of agriculture. The Japanese rice fields need 50 to 65 million cubic yards of water annually.

To get these fields to grow satisfactory crops each year it is not enough just to irrigate; they must be kept productive, especially in a country like Japan where the soil is acid and poor. One could quote here all that has been written about the Chinese countryside; most of the effort expended and a good quarter of the cost of working the land is represented by fertilizers. Some of these are natural and traditional: human and animal wastes, composts, used water (especially bath water), ashes, fish offal. The strong odors that are encountered on certain evenings in the open country or on the flat-bottomed boats laden with precious fertilizers that are seen plying the canals of the cities are evidence of the tenacity of the old customs. Industry came to the help of the farmer early in the century and produced various organic and inorganic fertilizers (fish, soybean meal).

With irrigation and fertilization, labor is the third element in the cultivation of the soil. For a long time it consisted simply of human effort, aided by a few implements which, like the swing-plow in the West, had not changed at all since the Middle Ages. Only in northern Honshu was the horse used, and then merely as a remount in the feudal armies. Elsewhere the basket, the tow-rope, and the tool with handle were the only objects used to help man cultivate the soil. Mechanization developed according to the limited needs of the small parcels of land. Hand tools multiplied and were followed later by gasoline and then electrically driven water pumps and threshing and winnowing machines. Plowing and harrowing, however, continue to this day to be done by hand in many places, as is planting, despite the use in neighboring China of ingenious machinery for this purpose. The first regions to become mechanized were the single-crop areas such as those in Hokkaido, where the biggest farms are found.

Problems Raised by Traditional Methods of Agriculture

The gradual substitution of the machine for hand labor came at the end of a long series of efforts, described in Chapter 1, to make the poor and inadequate soil attain maximum production. We have seen how the chronic scarcity of arable land affected the standard of living and even the population figures, until the industrial revolution in the Meiji period offered the rural population fresh opportunities. Today's 12.5 to 15 million acres of cultivated land (increases from new clearings and drainage were more than erased by the spread of urbanization) are divided among some 5.6 million farming families, an average of less than 2.5 acres for each family (as against 2.25 acres in 1971). Because of the number of large landed estates and the prevalence of usury, at the outbreak of the Second World War a good half of this land was in the hands of 7.5 percent of the real owners, while 7.5 million acres were worked by 68 percent of the rural families. Farm leases exacted payment in rice that often amounted to two-thirds of the harvest, and they could be renewed indefinitely.

In 1946 the laws were reformed at American insistence; the state bought up one-third of the cultivated land and resold it on easy terms to two million underprivileged families. Each one received full title to about 2.5 acres. Ten percent of the land was rented for a payment of nine percent or less of the harvest. However, the repatriation of colonists from Korea and Manchuria, in addition to the high postwar birth rate, considerably augmented the agrarian population. At the present time the Japanese land is overpopulated (averaging 12 to 15 persons per acre), and the acreage limits authorized by the reform (in general, 5 acres per farm) discourage mechanization.

The fundamental problem is what place to give to agriculture in the national economy. There are too many farmers and for too long they have been denied their proper share of the national wealth. Without question, this small landowner class, viewed in the light of the great changes that have occurred in the urban and industrial worlds, preserves a mode of life and a social structure that belong to the past and that will one day have to be eliminated. Unable to live entirely off the farm or to increase its size, the Japanese farmer devotes only part of his time to it. Of the 5.6 million farms, just one-quarter, 1.4 million, are worked full time, and half of the others, some 2 million, are only a secondary source of income to the occupants. The land is cultivated by the old and the young while the able-bodied, employed elsewhere, return to help in the busy periods. Exceptions are the pioneer front in Hokkaido and the market gardens where the difficulties and the great amount of work require the presence of all hands.

Up to the Second World War the main theme of Japanese agrarian policy was the need for the country to feed itself with the products of its own soil. The state began granting generous subsidies to the rice farmers and bought their crops at a fixed price. As a result, Japan became self-sufficient in rice, and the farming class enjoyed an increasing prosperity. This policy, however, which is still followed today, is costly, not only to the state but also to the majority of citizens in the urban centers. Rice, vegetables, and fruits cost more in Japan than in any other country, and this has led the government to question the policy. Imported rice and wheat are two-thirds the price of Japanese rice and wheat; sugar, one-half; milk and butter, 40 percent. Most agricultural products could be imported at lower prices. Basically it is the small size of the farm (2 million have less than 1.25 acres; only 63,000 have more than 12.5 acres), the archaic customs that prevail in farming, and the importance of rice in the Japanese diet that prevent the farmer from producing cheaply.

Thanks to state subsidies, the farmer has been able to raise his standard of living. Protected as he is against foreign competition, he begins to look more and more like a privileged person with a purchasing power that enables him to modernize his home and his fields. To his income from the farm he can add a salary from business or industry which leaves him well off and makes him, with the middle-class urban dweller, one of the two important markets for industrial products. The average farmhouse today in the more progressive areas has a corrugated tin roof, a refrigerator, a television set, and an automobile or small truck in the adjoining garage. Indoors, the fine polished woodwork has made way for tile floors and plastic materials, less esthetic but easier to take care of; in the winter, gas and electricity have replaced the traditional hearth.

The farmer uses part of his income to modernize his farm. The number of tractors and small hand tractors increased from 0.5 million to 3.5 million from 1960 to 1976, and other mechanized or motorized machinery from 350,000 to 3.5 million, or ten times the 1960 figure. The traditional neighborly practice of lending and the popularity of the cooperatives add to the significance of these figures. In 1960 it took 173 man-hours to cultivate one-quarter acre of paddy; by 1971 the same work could be done in 128 hours. For wheat, the labor was reduced by one-half. Therefore fewer hands were needed for greater productivity and higher market prices.

The price of food, however, remains a problem. The man in the city has become less willing to sacrifice his standard of living for the sake of a rural minority. A solution would be to reduce the number of farmers, to further mechanize the farms, and, in particular, to increase their size, but the land reform measures of 1946 preclude such expansion for the time being. A substantial change in agricultural production was the purpose of the Basic Agricultural Law of 1961. It proposed that, instead of continuing to raise crops that could be grown more cheaply elsewhere (rice, beans, potatoes, wheat, silk, sugar), Japan concentrate its agricultural efforts on high-priced products that were in increasing demand in the world. His growing prosperity has made the farmer familiar with modern ideas about productivity and profits, and he is showing a greater interest in such items as meat, fruits, green vegetables, butter, and cheese, all of which mark a new departure in Japanese agriculture. At the same time, the production of cereals (other than rice) is rapidly diminishing, as is that of sweet potatoes, soybeans, and rapeseed, which are now imported in increasing quantities.

From Rice Field and Farm to Pasture and Orchard

The transformation of the countryside is already apparent in many regions, but in different ways. The trees are probably the most startling intruders in the conventional landscape of rice paddies. Some of these plantings are very old—the teaplant, for example; others, like the mulberry, were planted within the past century; yet others became popular only before the Second World War. The mandarin orange, which is a winter fruit, is an example of the latter. It grows best on the hills surrounding the city of Shizuoka and on the neighboring Izu Peninsula, 65 miles south of the capital. Many hands are recruited to pick the fruit at harvest time, and they are assisted by an ingenious system of overhead cableways that carry the fruit down to the valleys. At the railheads, the large installations that check and pack the oranges are run by powerful cooperatives. In the ten-year period from 1960 to 1970, annual production increased from one to two million tons.

The apple orchards are in the Nagano (Chubu) basin and around Hirosaki at the extreme northern end of Honshu. They were not developed as intensively as the citrus fruits because they produce only one-third as much per acre. The peach orchards in the Kofu basin at the foot of Mt. Fuji and the pear, peach, and mandarin orchards in the Okayama district on the Inland Sea are also multiplying at the expense of the paddies.

Among all of these the grape vine has a place of its own. As a fruit, the grape is not new to Japan; its use for the production of wine, however, is of very recent date. About 280,000 tons are picked each year in certain special areas. It is grown especially in Tohoku (Yamagata), in Nagano and Okayama, and, last in importance, in Kyushu around Fukuoka. The wine industry has its vineyards in the Kofu basin, where they cover more than 12,500 acres. The vines here grow on trellises and average only six to eight slips per acre. They cover the borders of the plain and extend up the slopes where they keep encroaching upon the forest. The industry is in the hands either of large producers who have their own cellars or of cooperatives, formed by a number of small and medium-sized wine growers. Japanese wine is quite potable, and the producers are well informed about the industry in Europe, Australia, and the United States.

On the Pacific side, close to the orchards of Shizuoka or alternating with the rice fields in certain areas of Tohoku, Kanto, and Kansai, are a growing number of vinyl-covered hothouses in which vegetables and flowers are being raised. They are found also as far north as Hokkaido's Ishikari Plain, where they serve as nurseries for the rice seedlings, thereby gaining two weeks and sheltering the plant during this brief and delicate period of its growth. On the outskirts of Shizuoka, at the foot of the Nihon-daira plateau, vinyl also covers the espaliers of rock upon which strawberry plants have been trained to grow; they supply the Japanese market with strawberries the year round. On the slopes of Izu Peninsula and on the big island of Awaji that closes Osaka Bay to the west, flowers are raised in these vinyl hothouses. The flower cult, the art of flower arrangement, is a national tradition, and the taste for cut flowers is developing rapidly. Chrysanthemums, irises, roses, and carnations are on sale at florist shops the year round. But this kind of agriculture under cover is found mostly in market gardens, and wide areas on the outskirts of cities are covered with substantial hothouses of glass or lighter ones of transparent vinyl in which tomatoes, cucumbers, and lettuce are grown. Since the soil is well fertilized and the temperature and irrigation can be carefully regulated, four and five crops a year are possible. To give but one example: from 1960 to 1970 the tomato crop increased from 240,000 tons to nearly 1 million tons.

Fruit has been grown in Japan since ancient times, and market gardens and flower nurseries owe a great deal to the old tradition of gardening based on irrigation and intensive fertilization of the soil. Animal husbandry, on the other hand, is a recent activity which had its timid beginnings in 1960 as a consequence of the sudden prosperity of the farmer. It required a larger investment, of course, than the market garden or fruit orchard, and it developed only because planners saw that there was a market of sufficient importance to warrant the risk. The country lacked natural pasture land, and the average farmer was reluctant to exchange his paddy for fodder crops since he was guaranteed a good price by the government for his rice. Moreover, with no tradition to rely on (except the breeding of horses in Tohoku), he hesitated to adopt a type of agriculture which entailed such a profound change in his way of life. Yet when he did take it up it was done quickly, with substantial funds right from the start and with the encouragement of a powerful dairy industry that organized production and collection and of large sausage factories that helped finance the hog farmers.

Of all these animals the hog is the only one known since earliest times. The farmer turned to it first since it needs so little care, and today it can be found everywhere, on the Kanto Plain in Honshu, in Hokkaido, and in the southwest, in Kyushu, as well. Pork is the most popular meat in Japan, although it is not processed as well as in the West. The poultry industry also has grown rapidly and is now generally housed in buildings accommodating 2,000 to 3,000 birds each. But animal husbandry in Japan depends principally upon cattle and the milk, butter, cheese, meat, and fat they furnish. They are being raised on land hitherto unoccupied—on upland terraces, hills, and volcanic plateaus, as in southern Kyushu, which have been turned into pasture lands. The government has systematically aided this effort by importing pedigreed animals, especially Holsteins, and by offering generous loans to farmers planning to start a herd. Milch cows are particularly numerous in Hokkaido where 25 percent of the farmers are dairymen, but they are also raised in Iwate, in Tohoku, and near Tokyo and Kobe. Beef cattle, on the other hand, are concentrated in the west, in Hiroshima and especially in Kyushu, where one-third of the total number is found on the southern plateaus.

The government may have planned to diversify the products of the farm, and the farmer may have wanted to test new crops, but the profound change in Japanese agriculture could not have occurred without a parallel change in the daily diet of the people, and of the urban population in particular. Improvement in the standard of living has actually transformed the eating habits of the Japanese. The traditional diet was based on rice (only since Meiji; before then, rice was a luxury reserved for special occasions), pickled vegetables as a condiment, sweet potatoes and beans, and of course fish. A soup of *miso* (a fermented soybean paste) and rice with soy sauce were the chief items on the morning menu and still continue to be so in most of the countryside.

In the cities, however, milk and bread have almost replaced these breakfast dishes; at other meals, butter, cheese, meat, fresh or preserved fruit, and green vegetables are served regularly in homes or restaurants, where they are prepared as in the West or combined with food cooked in the traditional manner. The amount of meat consumed is only 22 pounds per capita per year (compared with 226 in the U.S., 176 in France, and 9 in India), whereas for fish the figure is 61 pounds (France, 15 pounds; U.S., 11 pounds). Fried chicken has become a popular dish but other kinds of poultry are rarely eaten. Milk is less common than in the West despite the fact that consumption has doubled in thirty years (3.5 ounces per person per day, compared with 26.2 in Denmark, 23.4 in the U.S., 20.8 in Britain, and 3.8 in India). Calories from animal food total only 11, as against 49 for France, 44 for the U.S., and 5 for India. The quantity of sugar used is still minimal: 1.8 ounces per person per day (U.S., 4.7; France, 3.2; India, 1.8). The consumption of fruit is increasing rapidly and in various ways: fresh, as juice, or canned, as in jams.

Appearing at the same time as these great changes in the eating habits of the people, the new methods of cultivation and new food products were meant to satisfy a domestic consumer market that was always looking for something new but still insisted upon quality (which is carefully watched by consumer groups). The Japanese economy has felt the impact. An important food industry that has organized every type of producer from the small workshop to the big milk companies now stands alongside the old factories that still turn out such traditional products as soy sauce and seafood. The meat and poultry industry and the wholesale distributors of fruits and vegetables now compete with old organizations that for centuries have transported rice from the plains of the north and northwest to the cities on the Pacific littoral as well as salt and fresh fish from the coast to the interior of the country. These busy, intricate exchanges between one end of the archipelago and the other best exemplify the new regional geography of Japanese agriculture.

The Great Agricultural Regions

Both the new and the traditional products of the farm are distributed unequally over the four principal islands, primarily because of the climate which makes it impossible for certain plants to grow in the north. While rice theoretically will grow up to the northern limits of the country, the sweet potato stops at the parallel of Sendai, 200 miles north of Tokyo; the mulberry stops a little further south, together with those plants that replace rice in the winter. Tea is not found north of the Niigata–Fukushima line, and the mandarin orange, which cannot bear the long winters on the Japan Sea coast, will thrive only on the shores of the Pacific and the Inland Sea. Man's long occupation of the archipelago is responsible for other regional variations as well. The basic food plants are found for the most part in the west, which has been inhabited for almost two thousand years. The central and northern zones, where unoccupied, arable land is still available, are favored by the new products, despite the fact that this is the best area for growing rice. And Hokkaido, the latest region to be settled and developed, has a distinctive rural appearance that reminds one not of the rice fields of Asia but of the agricultural areas of the "new countries" of the Far East, of Heilongkiang in northern Manchuria or the Siberian plains of the Lower Amur.

There is, to begin with, the central zone, the real heart of the country. It extends from northwest Kyushu to Kanto and is the land of the rice paddy. Here the plant is still grown according to ancient and intricate methods and only after elaborate preparation of the fields. Dikes are raised, the area divided into tiny irregular plots, irrigation channels prepared, buildings erected. The classic rotation of rice and dry cereals (wheat, barley) is supplemented by the sweet potato, the *igusa* (from which house mats are woven), or by dye-plants and plants for making paper. The climate here is mild, and the soil, which has been enriched by human labor, can be cultivated without interruption.

Within this ancient zone the regions vary according to climate and type of urbanization. Because of the heavy snowfalls in winter, only one crop a year is harvested on the northwestern coast (San-in and Hokuriku) where rice is grown exclusively. There are clusters of houses on the dikes in Niigata, dispersed farms hidden behind trees on the plains of Toyama, and both types of settlements in San-in; yet all are similarly surrounded by a sea of rice—green in the spring, golden in summer—that spreads to the very foot of the inland mountains.

Conditions on the Pacific slope, as we have already mentioned, are very different. Here an unbroken chain of cities provides an enormous consumer market. Rice is confined to the northern and central regions, leaving the plains free for higher-priced products that are shipped with difficulty, like mandarins, tea, vegetables, and flowers, while the hills and plateaus are given over to pasture lands for the cattle. Orchards and cattle farms, found along the Inland Sea and in certain parts of Kyushu, almost outnumber the rice fields that were once supreme. Nowhere in Japan, with the exception of Hokkaido, are hothouses more numerous, agricultural cooperatives more powerful and better organized, or agriculture itself so commercialized. Inland, rice fields are plentiful in the basins but orchards are beginning to intrude (apples in Nagano, peaches and grapes in Kofu), and cattle are now grazing on the plateaus. In the more distant valleys a traditional, if not archaic, way of rural life still exists, the farmer cultivating small burnt-over clearings or narrow fields dug out of the mountainside. On these heights, as well as those in Tohoku, the woodcutters and the charcoal burners live on lonely farms similar to those in the European Alps, which they work in summer and abandon in the winter.

Around this rural heartland of Japan extends a peripheral zone that was settled later and less densely. It developed on the northeast and southwest borders of the central zone and has an equally varied character and appearance. One region is remarkable for its climate. It lies within subtropical Japan and spreads over three areas: the southern end of the Kii Peninsula (in Kansai), southern Shikoku (Kochi and Tokushima), and Kyushu (Miyazaki and Kagoshima). We have already spoken of the climate of these plains and shores, of the heat and the heavy rainfall that make possible two rice crops a year. Inland, the mountains are exploited in a very primitive manner. This zone is not part of the ''heartland'' because it has remained outside the national economy and acquired modern agricultural methods very late and sparingly. One exception, however, is the cattle farms of northern Kyushu.

It is in northern Honshu in particular that the ''peripheral'' character of this rural economy is manifest. Here the land was settled relatively late, the population is small, and the growing season so brief that north of Sendai the fields lie fallow all winter. In the absence of a consumer market of any importance, most of the local products must find their way to the big cities of Kanto, Tokai, and Kansai. In northern Tohoku the paddies occupy 40 percent of the arable land (the national average is 65 percent); production, however, is superior to the national average. Wheat and other cereals figure prominently and crops from burnt-over clearings at one time were the most important in all Japan. Here as in the subtropical southwest can still be found some of the most primitive lifestyles of the archipelago. On Mt. Kitakami in Iwate the farms are scattered over slopes so steep they appear to be suspended between the sky and the valley below and are connected by footpaths that only men and beasts can climb. Horses are still used for transport and for the manure they provide. The primitive houses are in sharp contrast to the wealthy farmhouses on the plains below.

The latter, near Sendai, in the Kitakami valley, and around Yamagata and Akita, are surrounded by a vast expanse of rice fields that until the reform measures of

1946 were largely in the hands of a few wealthy farmers. Like those on the neighboring plains of Hokuriku, these farms send most of their produce to the great city markets of central Honshu. This commerce has opened up the region to new types of farming—to large orchards in Aomori and Fukushima, to vineyards in Yamagata, and to cattle raising in new villages in Iwate and Akita built in fresh clearings on the slopes of the central uplands. Here and there a modern farm appears with its silo, its corrugated-tin outbuildings housing modern machinery, its permanent stables. These become more numerous as one advances north and approaches Hokkaido.

Rural Hokkaido has a unique aspect because of its climate, the manner in which it was settled, and the "exotic" nature of its agriculture. Across Tsugaru Straits the change is striking: the immense pine forests, the roads lined with poplars, the orderly fences, the herds of cattle, all of this in a profusion unknown to the rest of rice-growing Asia. The average size of the farm (10 acres) is the highest in the country (compared with 2.25 acres for the whole country and as little as 1.25 acres in Kansai). The farmland itself is divided into great rectangles that extend for tens of miles. Distinctive are the farmhouses, many built of cement and flanked by a silo and outhouses; the many well-kept roads crowded with tractors, pick-up trucks, wagons, and horse sleighs in winter; the powerful group of companies supporting the food industry—everything here points to a type of rural community that is unique in the archipelago.

Another characteristic of the region is the range of its original products. Here also rice is the basic crop, and the farmer has shown great ingenuity in developing its resistance to the cold and compensating for its short growing season. The rice is grown on only one-fifth of the cultivated land; because of the immense size of the plains, however, this amounts to 500,000 acres. The extensive acreage, plus the high yield (2 tons per acre), produces 15 percent (800,000 tons) of the total for the nation. Beyond the limits of the Ishikari Plain, however, fodder-plants, sugar beets, turnips, and potatoes begin to be seriously cultivated. Cattle raising is popular and has become the dominant industry in the eastern region of Konsen. This particular area has one-quarter of all the Japanese milch cows and half of all the horses. Hokkaido, which at one time had 85 percent of the grazing land in the archipelago, still retains a greater percentage than any other region. Cattle can be stabled for long periods at a time thanks to the fodder that is gathered locally.

The Konsen region is the country's last frontier. Large clearings have been made in the open forest and linked to each other by long, straight roads that each year suffer serious damage from the spring thaw. The cold, the summer fogs, and the isolation make this region the most inhospitable in all Japan for the farmer. Dressed in his leather jacket, traveling over his land by jeep or on horseback, weighing every effort he makes in terms of profit or income, this farmer definitely represents a new type of individual in Japanese rural society.

The Exploitation of the Sea

WITH A harvest for 1975 of 10.5 million tons of sea products, Japan is slightly ahead of the second-place Soviet Union and well ahead of third-place China. In every period of its long history, Japan has looked to the sea for a large part of its food. In addition to the quantity it furnishes, qualitatively the sea supplies two-thirds of the animal proteins in the average diet, and although the present improvements in animal husbandry and the increased consumption of meat are steadily reducing this proportion, the demand for fish and shellfish continues to grow rapidly. Fish is eaten raw or cooked, along with other marine products like crustaceans, shellfish, and algae.

That the Japanese from early times have looked to the sea for their food is due undoubtedly to the scarcity of arable land. A further reason is the proximity of the coast to the inland plains, which allowed the taste for fish to spread throughout the country. As a result the Japanese have developed many traditional ways of life derived from this exploitation of the sea that, like those based upon the rice field, have made basic contributions to their control of the natural environment. The extraordinary economic progress of the country since 1868 and particularly in the 1950s is apparent even in this ancient industry, and here as on all the seas of the globe the Japanese fisherman is continually extending and modernizing his activities. To study the fishing industry, therefore, one must not only consider the shores of the archipelago but also the neighboring seas and the "global ocean" where the Japanese are always busily engaged.

Generally speaking, the natural conditions, while favorable, are in no way exceptional. They differ widely in the principal sectors: Pacific, Okhotsk Sea, Japan Sea, and Inland Sea. Everywhere, however, the violent winds (the winter monsoons of the Japan Sea, the typhoons in the East) render useless any of the natural shelters found along the rocky coast, and fishing villages are situated on the exposed beaches as well as in the bays and inlets. The ocean has one great gift to offer, nevertheless. Here, off the southern coast of Tohoku, the cold Oyashio current and the warm Kuroshio current meet and join. The junction of these two streams, each with its peculiar properties, encourages the growth of plankton, which in turn attracts great schools of fish.

The floor of this ocean is largely rocky and drops away suddenly to form great marine trenches not far from shore, thus restricting the area for trawling. The same problem occurs in the Inland Sea, where the presence of numerous islands and reefs makes trawling difficult. This method of fishing, however, is commonly used in the Okhotsk Sea, which has a relatively level floor, and is also popular, though less important, in the Japan Sea.

Those seas north and west of the archipelago are the natural fishing grounds of Korea and the USSR and have been the cause of several international disputes. Since 1945 Japanese boats have been forbidden to enter the territorial waters of these two countries. The USSR has denied entry to most of the Okhotsk Sea and every year there are tedious negotiations to determine the quota for each country, for crab and salmon especially. Confrontations between Japanese and Soviet fishermen in the waters off the Southern Kurils are likely to continue until the dispute over ownership of these islands is settled. Canada set the 175th meridian as the line beyond which Japanese ships may not fish, while the United States tries to keep Japanese fishermen from entering its waters, near Alaska in particular. The imposition of the 200-mile limit by both the United States and the Soviet Union has cut Japanese fishermen off from their best sources of fish, and it compelled Japan in 1977 to resort to the same measure to safeguard its own fishing grounds.

Traditional and Modern Fishing

Traditional fishing methods are still used off the coasts of Japan. Of the 200,000 enterprises exploiting the seas, about 80 percent are composed of a single fisherman's household, using a boat of less than 3 tons; of the 300,000 motored and motorless vessels they take to sea, 90 percent are under 5 tons. These small boats are of wood, and their construction shows few regional differences; all are typically Far Eastern. Thirty thousand families use boats of 3 to 10 tons. Those over 50 tons represent only 1 percent of the total number, although they are responsible for one-third of the annual catch.

The gear of the Japanese fisherman is extremely varied: single or multiple lines (trawl lines for tuna fishing); big nets of different shapes, some to be placed perpendicularly to the shore or simply anchored at one end; square nets for casting or for dragging, many of them resembling the equipment used in the West. Bait or lights serve to attract the fish. These nets are most often used to fish in shallow waters, to catch sardines and herring that stay close to the coast. This type of fishing is rather primitive, and per capita returns are only one-fifth those of the European countries. But since the 1960s, fishing methods have been rapidly modernized. Nylon nets, rotating seine nets, and longer and more sophisticated trawl lines are now commonly employed, while the trawlers themselves are being adapted to the needs of the different fishing grounds. They are increasing in tonnage, although usually still built of wood, and often stand 12 or 15 miles offshore to fish.

As in other areas of the Japanese economy, this modernization has taken place within the limits imposed by social and professional customs inherited from the past. The sea, more than the rice paddy or the forest, calls for a communal type of exploitation because of the risks involved—the actual dangers as well as the economic risks—and the amount of capital invested (a nylon net or a trawler can be very expensive). Even more than in the country village, each person here has his place in the strict economic and social hierarchy.

The cost of a boat and a new net has, since the beginning of the modern period, restricted ownership to the wealthy. In most fishing villages the means of production are concentrated in the hands of a very few, the *amimoto* (masters of the nets). These men live on the beach where they can keep an eye on the boats. They hire the fishermen, pay them according to their share of the catch or their seniority, and often lend them money, in this way adding the special relation of debtor-creditor to those obligations already mentioned in connection with rural life. They are present each evening when the boats return, and they watch the fish being unloaded and processed by still others whom they control in the same way. Thus the Japanese pattern of paternalism, seen in the relations between employers and employees in the great commercial companies, can be found as well in the family-like atmosphere of the fishing village.

The fishing villages differ widely in appearance. Some are perched on high cliffs, overlooking the sea, as in south Shikoku or Kyushu where the shores are swept by the cruel typhoons; others, on the Japan Sea, are built on dikes and the houses in winter are covered with mats of rice straw to protect them from the snow; yet others hide in the sand dunes as in Niigata or on the great Kujukuri beach north of Tokyo. With their backs to the cliff and facing the sea; their ground floors wide open to accommodate fishing boats; their roofs thatched (Kyushu, Hokkaido), tiled (Shikoku, Kyushu), or weighted down with loose rocks (on the Japan Sea); their walls that were once the weathered planks of a boat sheltered by some tall embankment (Okinawa, Shikoku)—they occupy every likely site and represent every type of traditional house.

In the village, life is centered on the beach. Here the fishermen gather at dawn, and here in the evening they pull up their boats. The day's catch is brought ashore, and late into the night, by acetylene light, the women stay behind to mend the nets. Here, too, are many different kinds of construction: simple shelters for the boats or, figuring prominently, the tall drying racks for hanging up the nets or suspending the rows of fish to dry in the wind. In certain localities, female divers gather on the beach before going out to sea, where they plunge to great depths (up to 65 feet) for seaweed and shellfish.

Very different are the methods and the sites used for commercial fishing. The industry is in the hands of a few big companies of which Taiyo Gyogyo, at Yaezu near Shizuoka, is an example. Each company has its fleet of ships, commanded by a factory-ship and served by a number of "catchers." Here again equipment determines the importance of the enterprise, and the picture presented by the port of Yaezu differs as much from the fishing villages described above as, for instance, a textile mill in Nagoya or Osaka differs from a village of traditional weavers. On three sides of the port stand huge hangars into which, each morning, the frozen tuna is unloaded by cranes from the holds of ships as large as any freighter. Close by the docks are the cold storage plants, the modern office buildings, the chandlers displaying nets and fishing tackle, and the special workshops, stamping the urban scene with the economic and technical character of the industry.

Between the large, highly capitalized companies and the traditional *amimoto* are intermediate organizations that have been slow in developing. In addition to the cooperatives, which have multiplied since World War II and which, by organizing the "average" fishermen, have almost replaced the *amimoto*, there are small companies using boats of only about 100 tons but equipped with modern fishing devices that bring in catches of commercial importance.

Of the 2,000 fishing ports in Japan the greater number are small and of the traditional type described above.

Very few are of the modern, Yaezu description, or even a combination of the two, like Misaki at the entrance to Tokyo Bay, or Ishinomaki near Sendai. Often fishing is but one of the many activities of the more modern ports. This is true of Nagasaki, on the head of a ria in southern Kyushu; of Tobata, a part of the Kitakyushu agglomeration on the Straits of Shimonoseki; and of Kitakyushu itself. This type of port is also found at the other end of the country, in the large coastal cities of Hakodate, Otaru, Kushiro, and Abashiri in Hokkaido, where an annual catch of 100,000 tons or more is only one of many activities.

Intensive fishing varies in importance in the different sectors off the Japanese coast. In the Japan Sea it thrives only in the southwest, around Tobata and Shimonoseki, while the rest of San-in and Hokuriku are still content to use the old-fashioned methods. This is true also of the Inland Sea, where the early fishing techniques were born and where the little ports scattered among the innumerable islands are further hampered by the polluted waters. In the far north the Okhotsk Sea is a busy fishing ground although it is closed for three months of the year during which it becomes a frozen waste. The ports of Wakkanai, Mombetsu, and Abashiri are used for crab, salmon, and other cold-water fish catches; their modern installations stand on the shore next to many little establishments still employing the old ways of fishing which in this northern island date from feudal times.

The Pacific littoral remains the most active area for offshore and deep-sea fishing and is the scene of many varied activities. Here, fishing is being rapidly modernized. The great ports of Yaezu and Misaki now send their fleets far out into the Pacific and Indian Oceans.

Further north, on the Tohoku coast, small fishing ports still compete with large modern companies like those at Choshi, Ishinomaki, and Hachinohe. In the cold waters off this coast the catch consists principally of saury, herring, and salmon from the north, while in the southern waters from Kyushu and Shikoku to Tokyo the trawlers look for anchovies and sardines.

Fish Breeding

Life on the coasts has suffered a grave crisis since World War II because the seabeds have been depleted by excessive exploitation and polluted waters. Schools of herring and sardine have seriously diminished; the herring catch in Hokkaido and north Honshu, for example, which in 1953 amounted to 250,000 tons, is today one-fifth that figure. Faced with these problems, the fishermen, whose living standard is low—well below that of the average rice farmer—cannot remain indifferent to the lure of the industrial centers. A fresh approach to the industry, therefore, has become urgent. This has been made at three different levels: the development of sea farming, the exploitation of global waters, and the modernization of the infrastructure.

The initial effort was directed toward building up the fish population by strictly limiting the catches and by stocking the fishing grounds from hatcheries that could produce tens of millions of fingerlings annually. Some hatcheries cultivated beds of mollusks; others built artificial reefs to encourage repopulation. Japan, for the first time in the world, adopted a new way of exploiting the seas by breeding fish instead of catching them in the traditional manner. Fish hatcheries have multiplied in carefully selected bays along the coast, where the young are now scientifically fed until ready for market. In 1968, 1,556 of these hatcheries produced 30,000 tons of fingerlings in tanks covering 1,618 acres. Since 1970 new species have been developed by these techniques, aided by a string of laboratories stationed along the coasts.

This type of controlled production is already an economic success with mollusks and seaweed. Seaweed is an important item in the Japanese diet, the average inhabitant consuming over four pounds a year. It used to be gathered on upright stakes, but today flat bamboo screens are used. Some 70,000 people are employed to collect about 140,000 tons a year, of which Tokyo and Ise bays furnish about one-third. In 1974, 7,000 oyster growers supplied 210,000 tons of edible oysters, and 4,666 growers harvested 117 tons of pearls, particularly in Kashikojima Bay, south of Nagoya, and around Nagasaki. Most oysters for the table are raised near Hiroshima, but they are also found in the far north in lagoons on the Okhotsk Sea, where long periods under the ice do not seem to affect either their growth or flavor.

Pink shrimp are raised in quantity in the Inland Sea and the waters further south. The Japanese method of cultivating them is being constantly improved, but it is already such a commercial success that it has been adopted abroad, and Japanese technicians are on loan to the United States, several nations of Black Africa, and France. Finally there are the eels, a highly regarded item on the Japanese menu. The increasing demand for them has multiplied their breeding grounds, which are mainly in Lake Hamana, on the Pacific coast north of Nagoya. Here they have even invaded the adjacent rice fields, which have been deepened and flooded, increasing total returns 15 and 20 times. Nevertheless, the demand is still not satisfied, and quantities of young eels are being imported. It is likely that new hatcheries will be established in foreign countries under Japanese management or that Japan will purchase greater quantities of foreign eels.

A second feature of the Japanese exploitation of the sea is its extension since 1960 to all the waters of the globe. The concept of the Global Ocean is already an economic fact to Japanese entrepreneurs; their fleets, rebuilt between 1945 and 1954, made great progress after 1960, especially in trawlers and tuna boats. Beginning in that year, Japanese companies established bases in the Pacific, the Indian Ocean, and the tropical Atlantic. By 1971 they were making catches of 210,000 tons, 125,000 tons, and 53,000 tons respectively. From the tropical latitudes in these oceans the Japanese fishermen in more modern ships of larger tonnage are now steadily moving north and south to more temperate seas; before long they will be independent of any foreign port of call.

The expansion of the Japanese fishing industry over the oceans of the world has resulted, paradoxically, in a revival of activity in the home ports; this, consequently, has hastened their modernization. The central and northern sectors of the Pacific coast have especially profited by these improvements. This is particularly striking in such modern centers as Kushiro in Hokkaido and Hachinohe in Tohoku, each of which handles more than 400,000 tons a year. It is even more apparent in other ports like Choshi, at the mouth of the Tone River, near Tokyo, where close to 30 million dollars was invested between 1963 and 1975, and in Ishinomaki, near Sendai. Both towns hitherto were of no great importance but are now giants of the fishing industry as a result of their new facilities. Even the old ports of Yaezu and Misaki are improving their records. More and more, the southern sectors and the Japan Sea are falling behind, and their share of the total catch is growing less. In this respect Japanese fishing appears to parallel industry; like the latter, it is concentrated in specific coastal areas which are developing at the expense of other areas. Should relations with China improve, however, this situation could change.

The fishing industry refrigerates and processes the products of the sea and of the hatcheries, turning out dried, smoked, and canned fish and the fish pastes to which the Japanese are so partial. Production is increasing rapidly, due to an insatiable domestic market. The steady improvement in the domestic standard of living has increased the demand for every type of commodity. The products of the fishing industry are no exception. A certain quantity of frozen tuna and canned goods is exported: tuna to the United States and Germany, salmon to Great Britain and Australia, and crab to the United States and Western Europe. These shipments, however, do not amount to more than three percent of Japanese exports. The fishing industry today actually employs only about one percent of the Japanese labor force.

7

Providing Energy
for Economic Power

SINCE 1945, the rapid development of Japanese industry has doubled the demand for power about once every five years. This increase is a bit greater than that of western Europe; in terms of coal consumption it amounted in 1976 to 310 million tons, making Japan fourth in the world after the United States, the USSR, and China. On a per capita basis the figure for Japan of 2.2 tons places it tenth, after the United States, Canada, Czechoslovakia, the two Germanys, Britain, Australia, the Netherlands, and France.

While the use of power has increased rapidly, it has also changed qualitatively. In 1950 coal supplied half the needs of the country, hydroelectricity one-third, petroleum and the old sources the rest. Ten years later petroleum had attained the same percentage as coal; by 1967 it had doubled. That same year, a consumption of power equal to 193 million tons of coal actually used only 67 million tons of coal, or one-third of the total; 113 million tons, or almost two-thirds, was petroleum. The production of hydroelectricity amounted to 10 million tons, natural gas to 3 million tons. Atomic energy

141

was just beginning to appear. Modern developments have tended to reduce the use of coal and hydroelectricity and to increase the consumption of natural gas and atomic energy. Power of thermal origin has a major share which is steadily growing; by 1975 that share was 76.6 percent for electricity.

This heavy demand for energy presupposes a coordinated government policy since most of the raw materials required to produce it must be imported. (Coal is mined in sufficient quantity, but its share in energy production is decreasing.) Ninety-nine percent of the petroleum is imported, as is the uranium, and natural gas will soon be imported from Siberia. In 1950 Japan imported less than 5 percent of its basic raw materials; in 1965 the figure was 50 percent, and today it must look abroad for 70 percent of its needs, petroleum alone amounting to 15 percent of total imports.

The need to protect the coal-mining industry, the gradual liberalization of imports, and MITI's (the Ministry of International Trade and Industry) strict control of the power companies have called for complex legislation on energy resources. Generally speaking, the policies are as liberal as those in the field of industry. But private initiative is very strictly controlled by MITI, which, for example, fixes the prices of petroleum products and determines the fates of the coal mines. In a larger context, the encouragement given to companies exploiting various resources (the oil fields of the Middle East, for instance), the commissions of inquiry on the economic development of the nation's coal mines and petroleum fields, the expansion of foreign trading contacts (particularly with the USSR and China), the help given in building the nuclear centers—all of these

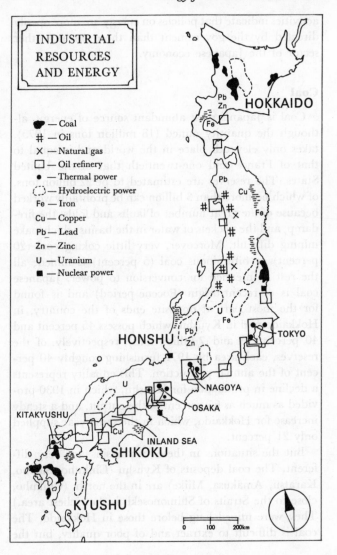

INDUSTRIAL
RESOURCES
AND ENERGY

- — Coal
- — Oil
- — Natural gas
- — Oil refinery
- — Thermal power
- — Hydroelectric power
Fe — Iron
Cu — Copper
Pb — Lead
Zn — Zinc
U — Uranium
- — Nuclear power

HOKKAIDO

HONSHU

TOKYO

NAGOYA

OSAKA

KITAKYUSHU

INLAND SEA

SHIKOKU

KYUSHU

0   100   200km

activities indicate that policies on energy are more openly directed by the government than those on any other sector of the Japanese economy.

Coal

Coal is Japan's most abundant source of energy, although the quantity mined (18 million tons in 1975), takes only eleventh place in the world and is equal to that of France and one-twentieth that of the United States. The reserves are estimated to be 22 billion tons, of which no more than 3 billion can be profitably worked because of the great number of faults and folds, the fire-damp, and the pockets of water in the basins which make mining difficult. Moreover, very little coking coal (20 percent) or bituminous coal (5 percent) is mined; all the rest is intended for conversion to power. Japanese coal is of recent origin (Eocene period) and is found for the most part at opposite ends of the country, in Hokkaido and in Kyushu, which possess 45 percent and 40 percent (8 and 7 billion tons), respectively, of the reserves, each area by 1971 furnishing roughly 40 percent of the annual production. This equality represents a decline in production for Kyushu, which in 1930 provided as much as 65 percent of the output, and a steady increase for Hokkaido, which in the same year supplied only 21 percent.

But the situations in these two basins are very different. The coal deposits of Kyushu (Chikuho, Sasebo, Karatsu, Amakusa, Miike) are in the north. (Chikuho, close to the Straits of Shimonoseki, is the richest area.) They were mined long before those in Hokkaido. The coal is difficult to extract and of poor quality, but the proximity of the mines to the sea facilitates transportation; also, the metallurgical and chemical industries of Kitakyushu can use the coal as a source of power. In Hokkaido the seams are wider (over three feet) and therefore can be worked mechanically, and the quality is the best in Japan. However, the mines are nearly 40 miles from the sea and even farther from the factories; the coal is shipped from the ports of Muroran and Otaru all the way to the industrial zone in Honshu. None of the other deposits in the nation are of equal importance. Joban, just north of Kanto on the Pacific Coast, and Ube, on the Inland Sea west of Hiroshima, are the largest. Honshu has total reserves of only 2.3 billion tons, and there is almost no coal in Shikoku.

The critical situation of these coalfields since World War II is due to old-fashioned methods of working the mines. In 1962, 501 mines supplied less than 100,000 tons each year, and only 8 produced more than 1 million tons. To extract the coal, the Japanese use inclined galleries instead of pits, extending them in places as much as six miles underground. This is a costly procedure, despite the recent installation of moving platforms. A miner's daily output in 1950 was only 0.4 tons a day, one-third that of a British miner and one-tenth that of an American. In 1962 MITI ordered a thorough study made of the industry; this led to the closing of the unproductive mines. In 1963 only 323 remained open (as compared with 703 in 1958), and the number of miners fell from 180,000 to 135,000. To avoid shutting down any more, it was decided to maintain the 1961 production figure of 55 million tons, but this could not be kept up for long. The mines still in operation today have been modernized at great expense; pits are replacing the galleries, and between 1957 and 1969 the area of the coal faces was doubled. Thanks to these measures, the output of the individual miner has increased in spectacular fashion and currently amounts to 1.3 to 1.5 tons per day.

This coal costs more than the imported product. Purchases abroad have increased, not because of the price difference but because the country produces so little coking coal. The latter constitutes approximately three-quarters of the coal purchases (about 44 million tons in 1975 out of a total of 62 million tons purchased). These are made mostly from the United States (43 percent), Australia (37 percent), and the USSR (10 percent). The Japanese steel industry has come to depend more and more on foreign coal, leaving the output of the national mines to pile up at the mouth of the pits. To absorb these stocks and at the same time to adjust domestic production to the industrial needs of the country, the government has developed sources of supply that lie inside the great manufacturing zone where they can furnish the necessary power. The Ube basin, conveniently situated in Chugoku's industrial region, is now the site of many chemical factories, and the Joban basin, the home of many different industries, has become part of the important urban complex north of Tokyo. In Kyushu, near Omuta, the shores of Ariake Bay are turning into one of the great carbochemical centers of the world. The Mitsui Company has invested heavily in this region; a steel mill and aluminum plant are already in production.

Most of the coal is converted into electric power. The government financed the construction of huge thermal centers in the principal coal-mining regions, offered loans at low interest rates to modernize plants, and encouraged mergers. These measures, in addition to the general economic progress of the country, have saved the coal mines. Moreover the demand for domestic coal in the carbochemical and electrical steel industries, and especially in the production of electricity for the national railways, should increase in the years to come. The labor problems also seem close to a solution. The serious cuts in personnel in the years 1958–64 have been offset by salary increases, by compensation for unemployed miners, and, more particularly, by the transfer of men to the new industries created in the mining regions.

Petroleum and Natural Gas

Although petroleum is in growing demand and already a major source of energy (65 percent), domestic production is a mere 0.8 percent of Japan's needs. Local wells supply less than 800,000 tons and are unequally distributed between the Akita fields (22 percent), which are almost exhausted, and those in Hokuriku, south of Niigata, which furnish three-quarters of the production. More promising is the natural gas from these same Hokuriku fields and from the area of Chiba near Tokyo, which provided about 7 billion cubic yards in 1975. This is more than double the energy supplied by petroleum. Pipelines for the gas connect Niigata with Tokyo.

Japan was tempted at first to prospect for oil herself in distant parts of the world like Sumatra and the Persian Gulf, but chose instead to lift domestic controls and import (262 million tons in 1975). This has made Japan competely dependent on others for crude petroleum, a fact that was brought to world attention during the 1973–74 oil embargo. Today, the oil comes principally from the

Middle East (Iran, 25 percent; Saudi Arabia, 26 percent; Kuwait and Abuh Dabi, 9 percent each). Oil imports from Indonesia have increased since 1933 (when Japan imported 42 million tons), because of Indonesia's proximity to Japan and Japan's unwillingness to rely solely on the Middle Eastern countries. China is another close source, and, despite the high sulfur content of Chinese oil, Japan imported 8 million tons (3 percent) of crude oil from there in 1975. While imports from the above countries are increasing, imports from the United States and Venezuela are down to almost zero.

Crude oil is brought by large tankers directly to the shores of the Tokyo and Kitakyushu industrial zones, where it is refined. Few of the by-products are exported (one million tons); they, too, are intended for domestic consumption. In capacity the Japanese refineries rank third in the world, after the United States and the USSR, and in 1976 they produced about 48.5 billion gallons. Nonetheless, Japan still must import about ten percent of the refined product, since its growing demands keep exceeding the capacity of its refineries.

Between the foreign sources of supply and the tankers (60 percent Japanese) that transport the oil, stand the big foreign companies that furnish about two-thirds of this petroleum, especially Caltex, Esso Standard of Japan, Tidewater, Gulf Oil, and Mobil. Their interests are principally in the refineries. Of the large Japanese companies in the industry, only Idemitsu Kosan is financially independent. In the others, the foreign capital invested is around 50 percent. (Caltex's interest is in Nippon Oil, Tidewater's is in Mitsubishi Oil, and Esso-Standard's is in General Sekiyu.)

The petroleum industry has stayed close to the refineries. A small part of it is located in the petroleum fields in Akita and Niigata on the shores of the Japan Sea, but the major installations are in the industrial zone and, within that zone, near the great cities. The Tokyo–Yokohama and Osaka–Kobe regions have refineries with a capacity of 40 to 50 million tons a year. Kawasaki, on Tokyo Bay, leads with 20 million tons, followed by Chiba, where new refineries are under construction. The others taken together equal the output of Yokohama. In the Kansai region the installations were erected in a more orderly manner between Sakai and Amagasaki. A third complex which supplies about 20 million tons is located on Nagoya Bay, at Yokkaichi and Tsu. Finally, along the Inland Sea, large refineries stand next to the big industrial plants, as in Mizushima (Mitsubishi), in Kudamatsu (Nihon Sekiyu), and Tokuyama (Idemitsu), each one supplying from 4 to 10 million tons. Across the sea on Shikoku, the most important refineries are Maruzen's at Matsuyama. The remaining 15 million tons are produced in smaller centers like Muroran and Hakodate in Hokkaido and the Akita–Niigata region. The latter area has a capacity for refining that in fact exceeds the tonnage extracted locally; this has attracted the chemical industry, which is proving a boon to this coastal area that is so poor in raw materials and sources of power.

Most of these installations are located on polders extending along the coast. The oil is brought directly to them from abroad, and then the by-products are treated in bulk—in plants at Kawasaki and Chiba–Goi on Tokyo Bay; Yokkaichi on Nagoya Bay; Osaka and Sakai in Kansai; Mizushima, Iwakuni, and Tokuyama in Chugoku; and Niihama and Matsuyama on Shikoku.

Electricity

Japan, with a total of about 475 billion kilowatt-hours in 1975, is the third largest producer of electricity in the world, following the United States and the USSR, but leading Great Britain, Canada, and West Germany. Of this total, the amount contributed by water power has been steadily declining and already in 1960 was surpassed by thermoelectric power. There were two reasons for this: the growing demand that could not wait for dams to be built, and the prohibitive costs of modernizing existing hydroelectric resources. This change has meant a growing dependence on foreign countries for the sources of thermal energy, especially petroleum, and has required special financing.

Beginning about 1930 the small private companies that were characteristic of the early years of Japan's industrialization started to merge, and by 1934 two large zaibatsu, Mitsui and Mitsubishi, were in control of 45 percent and 35 percent of the electrical industry respectively. In the military period that followed, the industry was nationalized, and in 1941 the Nihon Hassoden, a government body, took charge of production and transmission. This body was dissolved in 1951 and production turned over to private regional companies functioning under the supervision of the state. Nine such companies were established at the time; today they produce and transmit the bulk of Japanese electricity. A few individual producers such as the Oji Company (paper) in Tomakomai, Hokkaido, still exist; a state-owned company, the Dengen Kaihatsu, is constructing large installations throughout the nation, some of them in depressed coal-mining districts, and is selling power to the regional companies as well. The state also supervises the transmission lines, which need to be modernized (voltage loss on these lines during transmission is greater than in any other industrial country) and which have to be increased from 200,000 to 400,000 volts. The lines form a network across the nation, Hokkaido excepted, and are aerial between Shikoku, Kyushu, and Honshu.

The meager coal production and the scarcity of petroleum led very early to the development of hydroelectricity and particularly to a search for promising sites for the plants. If only domestic sources of energy are listed, hydroelectricity furnishes nearly 24 percent of the total—plus another 12 percent if imported petroleum is included. Although Japan is a land of mountains and heavy rainfall (summer rains everywhere, snow on the northwest coast), it suffers because its resources are divided among a number of small drainage basins that call for modest installations rather than the large or medium-sized power plants found on rivers in the USSR and even on the Rhine. It is handicapped further by the irregular flow of the rivers, the absence of mountain lakes of glacial origin, and the ground displacements and earthquakes which are a menace to its larger dams, which are also constantly threatened by the enormous quantity of debris carried by the streams.

For a long time only plants using water power were to be found on such obvious sites at Mt. Hida in the Japanese Alps or in the mountains of southern Tohoku. But by 1953 reinforced dams capable of resisting earthquakes were being built, and even arch dams were erected in certain secure areas. The most remarkable of these is Kurobe-4, at the northeast foot of Mt. Hida. An extensive network of highways and railway tunnels had to be constructed to transport workmen and material into the heart of this wild gorge. More large power stations are being built today in other parts of Chubu, particularly along the Shinano River. Tohoku ranks next in importance, followed by Kansai, but in all of Honshu the side facing the Japan Sea has always been preferable to the Pacific side for electricity production. In the west, the mountains of Shikoku, Kyushu, and Chugoku, although known for their heavy rainfall, are served by small rivers that cannot be profitably harnessed. These three regions provide 5, 7, and 5.5 percent respectively of the national output, but water power represents only 32, 20, and 16.4 percent of their total production of electricity. Finally, Hokkaido has several high, snow-covered mountains and uninhabited sloping basins where important installations were built after the problem of the cold had been solved. However, Hokkaido is not linked to the national network, and since it boasts a bountiful supply of coal, large plants are still relatively few; two-thirds of the power is of thermal origin. In fact, in every sector of the nation (except Hokuriku, where the figure is 68 percent), water power falls behind thermal power; even in Tohoku it amounts to only 47 percent of the total.

Thermoelectric plants therefore furnish the electricity used today in almost every part of the country. In 1935, 76.5 percent of the total power used was hydroelectric; the percentage was the same in 1955 because the generating plants, situated in sparsely settled areas, had been relatively undamaged by the war. By 1960, however, the figure fell below 50 percent and has continued to decline ever since. At 28.4 percent in 1967, it was around 23 percent in 1972 and will be down to 20 percent in 1980. Only 40 percent of the total hydraulic resources are in use today; the remainder are in remote corners of the country, in river beds incapable of supporting dams or in which the flow of water is too irregular, making the cost of the energy prohibitive. In all Japan, Kanto has exploited its resources to the greatest extent (70 percent of the total), followed by Kansai; this is due to the presence of big cities in those areas. Other regions use less than half their resources. This is true even of the mountainous regions poor in coal like Tohoku (48 percent), Chubu (46 percent), or Hokuriku (38 percent). Hokkaido, which lives off its coal, uses only a third of its resources.

Thermal power stations can be built rapidly and have greatly improved their technical facilities since World War II, but in Japan they enjoy yet other advantages. To begin with, both the coal-mining areas (Joban, Kitakyushu, Miike) and the storage tanks for imported petroleum are located on the coast; with the sea close by, costly water-cooling plants can be eliminated. Also, since consumer industries are concentrated in much the same areas, there is little loss in transmission lines.

Japan depends more and more on massive imports of petroleum for the production of electricity, and her generating plants use an increasing amount of heavy oil. This development was delayed until about 1964 by the need to protect the coal industry. Today only in or near the coalfields of Ishikari in Hokkaido, Ube, Ariake Bay, and Kitakyushu is coal the major fuel consumed. Regions lacking in coal like Chugoku (except for Ube, Shikoku, and especially the great conurbations) burn crude oil almost exclusively in their big power stations built close to the sea. There are stations at Himeji near Kobe, at Amagasaki and Sakai near Osaka, at Tsu and Yok-kaichi on Ise Bay, and very prominent ones on Tokyo Bay, the entrance to which is marked by the tall chimneys of the power plant at Yokosuka and the more recent one at Chiba across the way.

Except for Hokuriku, the electrical capacity of all these regions parallels their thermal capacity. Kanto heads the list with more than one-quarter (27 percent) of the 475 billion kilowatt-hours (79 percent of thermal origin), followed by Kansai (23 percent of the total, 74 percent thermal), then Chubu (15.5 percent, 62 percent thermal), Tohoku (8 percent and 60 percent), Kyushu (7 percent and 80 percent), Chugoku (5.5 percent and 83.6 percent), Shikoku (5 percent and 68 percent), and finally Hokkaido (4 percent and 64 percent). Hokuriku alone (4 percent of the total, 32 percent thermal) favors hydroelectricity. A further reason for the gradual decline of hydroelectricity is undoubtedly the dawning significance of nuclear power.

Japan's Nuclear Policy

The brief history of Japanese atomic energy falls into two periods: one of research, before 1970, marked by the construction of weak and quasi-experimental power plants; and the period after 1970, when electricity from atomic sources began to be profitable. For emotional reasons that are easy to understand, the Japanese hesitated a long time before creating nuclear power on their own soil, however peaceful its intended use.

A further reason for the delay was the relative scarcity of raw materials; the amount of uranium oxide in the archipelago will suffice only for a few years. Intensive prospecting has uncovered to date an estimated 10 million tons of mineral with an average of 0.052 percent uranium content; of this, 2.2 million tons have over 0.1 percent. These strikes are mostly in the interior, at Ningyotoge (50 percent), in Tottori, and in Tono (35 percent), north of Nagoya. The paucity of raw materials does not seem to disturb the Japanese; they plan an increase in the percentage of electricity of nuclear origin from 4 percent in 1970 to 16 percent in 1980 (or about 25,000 megawatts), 30 percent in 1985, and 50 percent by the year 2000.

Most of the uranium comes from Canada, which has agreed to supply 30,000 tons of uranium oxide ("yellow cake") over a period of years. In 1971 a contract was signed with France for the purchase of another 6,000 tons. The Japanese have already imported from South Africa, third in production among the nonsocialist countries, and are planning to buy in Australia. Their requirements are enormous if they are to realize the production figures mentioned above. They will need 9,000 tons in 1980, 21,000 tons in 1990, and by the year 2000 they will have had to import a total of 420,000 tons of uranium oxide. It is doubtful whether any purchases will be made in the USSR; until now the Soviets have merely offered to enrich minerals of non-Soviet origin.

In Japan the nuclear industry has developed in a manner totally opposite to that of other countries, where it is closely controlled by the government. Here it has been in private hands from the very beginning, and the first reactors, the ones imported from the United States in 1960, were bought by Japco, a private company established for that purpose. The government intervenes only to aid research or to coordinate. It does this through two governmental agencies known by their English names: the Japan Atomic Research Institute at Tokai-mura in south Tohoku, whose functions are pure and applied research; and the PNC (Power Reactors and Nuclear Fuel Development Corporation), which studies the powerful reactors and prepares plans for the nation. The PNC does not build nuclear power stations; it merely investigates new procedures and new ways of extracting uranium oxide from the raw material in an effort to become independent of American techniques and of the unsuccessful methods which were introduced by the British in the beginning at Tokai-mura. Ninety percent of the PNC budget is defrayed by the government; the balance is furnished by private companies.

Besides Japco, the private enterprises are the nine regional power companies mentioned in connection with the conventional sources of electricity. They built the nuclear power stations and with their own funds purchased the reactors from the United States (the only country supplying enriched uranium oxide). Another group of five companies specializes in manufacturing the many components of these power stations: reactor vats, now even sold to the United States; turbines and alternators for transforming the heat generated into electricity; a further processing of the refined uranium from the United States (especially by Sumitomo); buildings; pumps, etc. Research is conducted in a dozen government institutes, a few private groups, and the large universities, which sometimes have laboratories equipped with working reactors.

As in other branches of the Japanese economy, it is difficult here to distinguish or analyze the parts played by the government and by private industry. MITI seems to be responsible for general plans covering the country's requirements in energy, but the private companies, assembled in a body called JAIF (Japan Atomic Industrial Forum) representing some 360 companies, also draw up plans on a national scale. The members distribute the tasks on a basis of both competition and co-operation that is certainly one of the secrets of Japan's astonishing success. These private companies enter into contracts with foreign nations: with Canada and other countries for their raw materials, with the United States for reactors and enriched fuel, and with still other nations, making it possible for Japan's nuclear industry to keep abreast of advances in the field in any part of the world. In 1974, for example, a plant at Tokai-mura to reactivate radiated fuel was built on contract with the French company Saint-Gobain.

A chart of the work in progress and in prospect shows a well-balanced distribution of nuclear power stations throughout the archipelago. In late 1971, 3 were already active: Tokai-mura, Mihama I in Kansai, and Tsuruga on Wakasa Bay. Japan now has 12 nuclear reactors in operation for power generation. Sixteen others are in trial operation, under construction, or planned. By 1980, a total of 58 power stations will be under construction or in operation, about two-thirds of them built by the two regional companies of Tokyo and Kansai. There will be 2 in Hokkaido, 4 in Tohoku, 3 in Chubu, 4 in Kyushu, 1 in Shikoku, and 6 in Chugoku. The annual increase in nuclear electricity will average about 10 percent. By 1980, consequently, 16 percent of the power produced will be of nuclear origin, 20 percent hydro-electric, and 64 percent from conventional thermal sources.

+ **8**

The Role of Industry

ALTHOUGH Japan arrived late on the scene, it had secured an important place for itself in the ranks of the great industrial nations well before the Second World War by virtue of its command of the most modern techniques, its enterprise, and an efficient organization inherited from the past. Displaying a dynamism unique in the modern world, Japan began in the 1950s to accelerate its progress and before long had outdistanced the nations of Europe, taking a place close behind the United States and the USSR. Between 1960 and 1966 it doubled its productive capacity, and until 1972 its annual growth rate exceeded ten percent, about three times that of any European nation.

However, while the chemical and heavy metal industries and the endless convoys of tankers and ore carriers that supply them have multiplied since the war, the textile and foodstuff industries have been slowly declining, and behind the proud modern façade Japan presents to the world there still exist any number of primitive and antiquated manufacturing methods. On the outskirts of its cities are nineteenth-century workshops, and in

158

towns and villages handicraft centers continue to employ the patient and artistic skills of an earlier day in order to please a consumer market equally loyal to the past. From the traditional potter or papermaker to the polders studded with giant furnaces and cracking towers, the world of Japanese industry displays every type of production. For this industry did not develop gradually; it advanced in spurts, each time leaving intact some vestige of the past.

The General Condition of Industry

In 1868, Japan was a country of handicrafts like the rest of Asia. The Meiji government decided to give the nation modern industry, but not at any cost; the government wanted to provide the country with the means to thwart the imperialistic designs of the Western powers who were moving into Eastern Asia at the time. To defend itself, Japan would have to be equally powerful, and for this it would need to borrow from the Western nations what it took to be the source of their strength: modern manufacturing methods. It was, therefore, in the name of ancient ideals and with manifest patriotism that Japan started off on the great adventure.

Lacking capital and technical personnel, the government began by importing both and, starting at the beginning, built a double network of railway and telegraph lines to bind the country together. At the same time, it exploited its only known source of energy, the coalfields of Kyushu and Hokkaido. Near the first of these, at Yahata, the great steel industry was founded in 1901. In the years from 1870 to 1914 the government inspired the establishment of many manufacturing and commercial enterprises. It had to take the initiative because of the scarcity of private capital, and only after the enterprises were on their feet and viable were they entrusted to individuals judged capable of managing them. Since the country had limited resources, the government borrowed from abroad and at the same time developed the agriculture of the country, the only source of wealth it had to export. (At one time raw silk represented almost half of the nation's purchasing power.) The great merchant families of Mitsui, Mitsubishi, Sumitomo, and others were headed by able men who took advantage of the protection of the state to assert their power. These zaibatsu paid low wages to workers recruited from the overpopulated countryside and steadily extended their activities, controlling every step in both the production and distribution of the goods they manufactured. They were able from the beginning to take over the financial and commercial bases of Japanese industry, and the great success that industry achieved became their own personal success.

The period from 1880 to 1931 represents the first phase of this industrialization. It was marked by the emerging power of the zaibatsu and the nation's conquest of a vast and profitable colonial empire (Taiwan, Korea, Manchuria) rich in raw materials and markets. This was the golden age of textiles, of raw silk and cotton goods. During the First World War, the markets of Asia were left to the Japanese, and they took advantage of the situation to entrench themselves. In 1932 the military took over and gradually armed the country; before long, heavy industry had reached the level of the textiles, and the important chemical industry was started. After 1937 the conquest of north and east China was followed by intensive development of the mining resources of those regions, which, added to the resources in Korea, made Japan relatively self-sufficient in coal and minerals. However, the bombardments of 1941–45 destroyed about one-third of all the Japanese installations, and in the following years, during the Allied occupation, the zaibatsu were dissolved and Japanese industry put under strict supervision.

The Korean War in 1952 gave Japan's industries new life, ushering in the third industrial period, which continues to this day. During these years, the heavy metals and the petrochemicals reached their full development, and the total income from industry surpassed for the first time the income from agriculture. The former zaibatsu concentrations were revived in various ways. This time, however, while still encouraging foreign trade, industry began to channel most of its products into the domestic market that was now important and profitable.

Japanese products had attained international standards in quality and were well received in all the advanced countries of the world. This was the heyday of Japanese industry. From 1950 to 1973 the petroleum refineries increased their capacity from 2 to 205 million tons; the production of steel rose from 5 to 96 million tons, of aluminum from 25,000 to 1 million tons, of electricity from 45 to 450 billion kilowatt-hours; cement production was multiplied by 10, that of sulfuric acid by 5, the tonnage of ships built by 40. Concurrently, household goods were turned out at an astonishing rate. Refrigerators multiplied by 700; tape recorders by 12,000; television sets rose from zero to 10 million units. Each year since 1952, 20 to 30 percent of the national income has been reinvested in production. Figures like these have won for Japanese industry the exceptional position it holds in the world today.

No less remarkable than the evolution of this industry is its present-day character. In addition to being largely dependent upon the rest of the world, it has peculiarities that set it apart from the industries of other nations, chiefly the survival within its own framework of so much that belongs to the past. What is known as the "dual structure" of Japanese industry is the coexistence of powerful groups: the Japanese equivalent of trusts and combines, and factories of the old type. The latter, though they employ less than ten workmen each, still constitute 70 percent of all Japanese business enterprises.

Among the former are the zaibatsu. They have resumed their positions of power in almost every important economic organization of the postwar period. Reviving the names of Mitsui, Mitsubishi, Sumitomo, and so on, they have gone into banking, the metallurgical and chemical industries, transportation, and commerce, and have also formed numerous affiliates. Competition among them is intense; nevertheless, they remain in close contact and often cooperate, as in the great petrochemical and steel combines which they set up jointly in the new industrial zones on the Pacific coast. All of these big companies are integrated vertically. Mitsubishi, for example, imports iron ore in its own bottoms and turns it into steel in its Tokyo plants, then makes it into steel plates and bars in its Kawasaki factory. These steel products are then used, for example, to erect the towers of the cracking plant at the Mitsubishi petrochemical plant at Yokkaichi (which is known among other things for its synthetic fibers, woven in Mitsubishi factories at

Nagoya) and are also exported in ships built in one of the Mitsubishi yards at Nagasaki, Yokohama, Kawasaki, or Hiroshima. Since the war, independent companies of equal stature but restricted to a limited line of products have joined the zaibatsu as members of Japan's large-firms group. Idemitsu (petroleum), Matsushita (electrical appliances), and Sony (radios, television sets) are among the more prosperous.

The revival of the zaibatsu is due to the tendency in Japanese industry today to collaborate or merge. Because of the antimonopoly laws, companies planning to combine must first secure the approval of the Fair Trade Commission. The Commission receives as many as a thousand of these requests a year—about one hundred of them, since 1967, listing combined capital assets of over one billion yen.* Most of these mergers seek to reconstitute some powerful prewar group such as Nippon Steel (combining Fuji and Yahata) or the former zaibatsu. The latter are reforming the old associations that had been disbanded by the anticartel laws. The Mitsubishi group, for example, started anew by setting up Mitsubishi Shoji to handle trade in general, then merged three heavy metal companies in 1964 to form Mitsubishi Heavy Industries. The latter, in turn, drew close to Mitsubishi Electric, while certain big wire manufacturers and petrochemical companies sought to reach an understanding, also within the Mitsubishi orbit. Similar movements are taking place within the Sumitomo and Mitsui groups, although the latter combine has never been as important as Mitsubishi in metallurgy and heavy

*One billion yen is roughly the equivalent of $3.5 million (based on the normal range of fluctuation of yen value, from 300–270 yen per one U.S. dollar).

chemicals, and it lacks a central unit around which the organizations can grow.

In the steel industry, the most spectacular development in the past few years has been the merger of the Fuji and Yahata companies which, in 1970, revived Nippon Steel. The avowed object of the merger was to coordinate investment plans and manufacturing procedures and to economize in transport and distribution. Yahata and Fuji in 1969 were the two largest steel-producing firms in Japan and ranked fourth and fifth respectively in the world. The way the merger was effected is a good example of the spirit in which these negotiations are handled in Japan. Both company presidents met at one of the big Tokyo hotels in 1968, accompanied by about one hundred advisors. Shigeo Nagano, president of Fuji, then approached Yoshihiro Inayama, president of Yahata, and said, "We have a proverb that says, 'Don't cut down a living tree.' I believe it's time to take care of the tree." The Fair Trade Commission twice refused to give its approval before it finally consented. With sales figures in 1970 of $2.5 billion, the new company has moved ahead of Bethlehem Steel and ranks second in the world behind U.S. Steel.

Alongside these giants that employ 500 to 2,000 workmen in any one plant are a great number of factories with fewer than 100 workmen. The latter constitute 54 percent of the industrial labor force employed in 97 percent of the 581,000 manufacturing companies registered in the nation (as against 26 percent in the United States and 20 percent in West Germany). At the other extreme, factories with more than 1,000 workmen form 0.1 percent of the total and employ only 16 percent of the labor force (compared with 30 percent in the United States, 36 percent in West Germany). This illustrates the dependence of big industry in Japan on small establishments.

Most of the small establishments work under contract for the big industrial companies, supplying parts for radios and cameras, for electrical appliances, bicycles, and cars, which the big companies then assemble in their large factories. This system gives Japanese industry great flexibility and makes it possible to effect quick changes in a manufactured article.

Methods of work, however, differ considerably. In the small workshop productivity is poor, salaries are low (in 1960, 50 percent lower on the average than in factories employing over 1,000 workmen), and an exaggerated paternalism subtly exploits the excessive manpower; in the big companies, on the contrary, the lack of skilled labor has led to the rapid development of automation.

One of the advantages of this system to the product is, of course, the low cost of the finished article. It is this traditional organization of Japanese industry, originally based on abundant rural labor, submissive employees, and backward and ineffectual labor unions, joined with a skillful integration of all the stages of production and merchandising, that has made it possible for Japan to retain for such a long time a dominant position in the markets of the world. Since 1952, however, the situation has been slowly changing. Each year a number of the smaller companies have disappeared, and the scarcity of skilled workmen has driven up salaries. The repeated demands of labor unions, often resulting in local or general strikes, and a growing dependence on foreign ships for import and export have progressively curtailed all the early advantages.

A third characteristic of Japanese industry is its

dependence on the rest of the world for raw materials. We have already noted the foreign origin of many of Japan's sources of energy; the same is true of its raw materials. Japan produces neither cotton nor wool, and only 10 percent of its iron ore in small mines of meager output, situated for the most part in Hokkaido and Tohoku, where the Kamaishi mine is the most important (59 percent of total production). There are also some ferrous sands. Other metals—copper, lead, zinc—are more plentiful, but the mines, mostly in Tohoku, are widely dispersed. Gold, tungsten, chrome, molybdenum, and vanadium are mined, but in limited quantities. In short, half the copper and most of the iron ore, manganese, nickel and cobalt, salt and phosphates have to be imported. The nation is also short of coking coal. This situation, which makes Japanese industry dependent upon world resources, and the additional fact that all of the nation's metropolises with their capital and labor markets are found on the seaboard, explain the almost total concentration of industry in the coastal belt. These handicaps, however serious, have not discouraged the development of every type of modern manufacturing.

The Principal Industries

Based upon value added, Japanese industry can be divided into the following sectors: heavy metals (15.9 percent), tools (32 percent), chemicals (12.5 percent), textiles and foodstuffs (8.5 percent), china and glass (5 percent), and miscellaneous light industries (18 percent).

It would be more interesting, however, to classify these industries according to their organization and location. On this basis, they can be grouped into four major categories: (1) the nonmineral industries, found on top of their own raw materials (lumber, paper, fishing); (2) heavy industry (metal and chemicals), usually situated on the coast near the available facilities for transporting imported raw materials; (3) the mechanical industries in which labor is the determining factor (automobiles, for example); and (4) light industry (textiles, furniture, printing, etc.), generally found at the center of the labor and consumer markets.

NONMINERAL INDUSTRY

The first category groups those activities that are situated mainly on the seashore (fishing), in agricultural areas (food products), or in the forests. The paper and cellulose industries are examples. Until the Second World War the island of Sakhalin was the source of the raw materials; with the loss of the island in 1945, all activities were transferred to Hokkaido, where the largest manufacturing centers are found today, particularly the huge paper agglomerations of Ebetsu and Tomakomai, the home of Japanese newsprint. The foodstuff industry also falls into this category, often being located some distance from the big cities; for example, the dairies of Hokkaido, the fruit canneries of Tokai and the Inland Sea, and the wine cellars of Chubu. The size of the establishments varies greatly, from small drying sheds for fish to the great complex at Tomakomai, but they belong in the same category because they process nonmineral products on the very site they are found. In value added, they represent 15 percent of industrial production.

HEAVY INDUSTRY

The second group contains the heavy industries, the

metals and chemicals, the glass and ceramic industries. The locations of large plants in this category are determined by the need to import most raw materials and the coal and petroleum which are their sources of power. The semifinished products of these factories (steel products are an excellent example) are also transported by sea, either to the metropolitan centers where the manufacturing process is completed or directly abroad.

Japan's production of steel is often cited as a symbol of her industrial power. The progress of that industry has been spectacular. From 5 million tons in 1950 production rose to 96 million tons in 1973, and to 101 million in 1975. Before World War II the figure was less than 10 million tons. Thus Japan has become the third greatest producer of steel in the world, overtaking West Germany in 1963 and approaching the United States and the USSR.

The industry started in 1901 when the government built the first steel mill near the fishing village of Yahata on the Straits of Shimonoseki; this site was not far from the coal fields of Chikuho in northern Kyushu where there were also some iron-ore deposits. It grew rapidly, especially in the 1930s with the encouragement of the military, and reached its first peak during the war years. Three-quarters of the industry was destroyed by wartime bombardments, but by 1963 the Yahata mills were operative again and turning out six million tons, or one-fifth of Japanese production. Meanwhile, other companies had been established: Fuji, Nippon Steel, Kawasaki, Sumitomo, Kobe Steel; these, together with Yahata, furnished two-thirds of the nation's pig-iron and three-quarters of the finished steel.

More than in any other country, the steel industry in

Japan has had to coordinate its activities in order to overcome the serious handicap of an insufficient supply of raw materials. The mills have to import almost every ton of coking coal and iron ore they use. They have invested in mines in Malaysia, Brazil, the Philippines, Pakistan, Rhodesia, and India, and have contracts with Great Britain and the United States for these supplies, buying enormous quantities from them every year. One-half the iron ore from abroad comes from Malaysia and India, each furnishing about 22 percent; one-quarter is provided by Latin America, by Peru and Chile in particular, and almost one-fifth from Australia, whose share is increasing the most rapidly. Coking coal comes from the United States, Australia, Canada, and the USSR, but these imports are costly. The cost of the raw materials used in manufacturing one ton of steel was estimated in 1962 to be $40 as against $37 in West Germany and the United States. To overcome this serious handicap the Japanese companies learned very early to combine their efforts. One result was the merger in 1970 of Fuji and Yahata.

Rationalization of the methods of production has been greatly facilitated by the very size of these enterprises and has been proceeding systematically since 1952. The Japanese steel industry suffered severely during World War II when 32 of the 35 blast furnaces and 186 of the 206 Martin furnaces were destroyed. The three five-year plans of 1951, 1956, and 1961, which included projects to revive the steel industry and make it competitive in the world market, made it possible to reorganize the industry completely and increase production. Rapid technological progress was the result of thorough studies made all over the world. The United States provided the model for the giant blast furnaces, and the industry later borrowed from Soviet technology. Australia furnished oxygen converters. Between 1951 and 1953 the quantity of ore necessary to produce one ton of steel was reduced by 23 percent, coking coal by 38 percent. The use of oxygen and the process of heating by injecting heavy oil to hasten fusion helped to obtain this substantial economy in fuel. Today 75 percent of Japanese steel is produced in oxygen furnaces as against 40 percent in the United States. These improvements have increased production per man-hour and reduced labor costs. In Japan the cost of labor in 1972 for one ton of steel was $23 as compared to $38 in West Germany and $86 in the United States.

This expansion was made possible by loans. Up to 73 percent was borrowed, placing a very heavy burden on the industry. (The big American steel companies, it should be noted, finance 75 percent of their expansions with their own funds.) The local companies receive no government assistance. They must therefore borrow, and their attitude toward these loans is peculiar to them. They do not hesitate to assume long-term debts, gambling on the future with an optimism that, so far, has been fully justified.

The sites of the big steel plants were chosen for practical and economic reasons: 83 percent of the industry is situated in the manufacturing belt. The first steel mills were erected on the Straits of Shimonoseki; others were built on top of mineral-ore deposits, as at Kamaishi on the Pacific coast of Tohoku, or close to coal, as in Muroran, not too far from the coal fields of Ishikari in southern Hokkaido. However, all of these mills still had to import a large part of their iron ore and coking coal. This is even more true today, and the new steel mills have found it necessary to be near the sea where both ore and coal can be brought to them directly by ship. This reduces transportation costs, and on the land the companies reclaim from the bays they can build the docks they need and erect blast furnaces and electric furnaces close by. They have settled for the most part on the big industrial bays of Tokyo, Osaka, and Nagoya, but some of the more recent and more important installations, like those at Mizushima and Kashima, are on the southern coast of Tohoku and on the Inland Sea, areas that once were strictly rural.

The same conditions pertain to the chemical industry, which is also dependent upon imported raw materials and whose plants are consequently situated mainly in areas close to the sea. Until 1955 the industry specialized in carbochemicals and the production of colors, pharmaceuticals, and certain other products that are still important today: fertilizers, polymers for textile fibers, insecticides, and varnishes. To these it has added oxygen for the new steel mills. The factories are located on the coalfields of Chikuho and Miike in Kyushu, of Joban in Tohoku, and of Muroran, or near the steel mills on Tokyo and Osaka bays, at Mizushima and Kitakyushu. The electrochemicals form another group that is found in Hokuriku on the Japan Sea coast, near the mountains in the Nagoya region, and on Shikoku, where the Sumitomo Company has developed a vast complex at Niihama. Other isolated centers exist in Kyushu, particularly at Nobeoka and Omuta.

Finally we come to the petrochemicals, the pride of the Japanese chemical industry. Their importance dates from 1955. That year, the first five-year plan called for construction by the zaibatsu of four great centers for refining petroleum. Mitsui's was built at Iwakuni, Sumitomo's at Niihama, Mitsubishi's at Yokkaichi, and Nippon's at Kawasaki. Later, additional plants were constructed in other parts of the country. All are located on the waterfront—in Tokyo, Nagoya, and Osaka bays; on the shores of the Inland Sea; and on the Straits of Shimonoseki. They manufacture many synthetic fibers—polythene, polystyrene, polyethylene—which their research laboratories are constantly trying to improve. They also produce synthetic rubbers; plastic materials for industrial use that are now replacing the wood, clay, and metal commonly used in the construction business; tubing; toys; and tableware. The chemical industry constitutes 12.5 percent of total industrial production and the percentage is steadily increasing.

MECHANICAL INDUSTRY

The third group of Japanese industries makes tools—a term used in the broadest sense, for it includes not only machinery but vehicles and other metal products. In these industries, intricate manufacturing processes require many man-hours of work per unit of weight of the finished product. The factories depend largely upon the labor market and are therefore found either near or within the great urban centers. Automobile plants and shipyards are prime examples of this type of industry.

In the production of automobiles Japan ranks fourth behind the United States, West Germany, and Great Britain. In pleasure cars alone it overtook France in 1964, Great Britain in 1966, and West Germany in 1967. Of the 7 million cars—4 million of them light automobiles—that came off the assembly lines in 1975, about one-third were from the Toyota factories, where production, equal to that of the German Volkswagen, puts the Japanese company in third place in the world behind General Motors and Ford. Nissan, the second biggest manufacturer (1.9 million cars) is followed by Mitsubishi, Toyo Kogyo, Honda, and Fuji. In 1969 the country exported about 1 million automobiles, 400,000 of them to the United States alone. In 1975 the figure increased to 2.5 million. Southeast Asia is the second biggest market, Europe the third. The rapid growth of the industry is a recent phenomenon. Japan's first two automobile factories were started in 1933 by Toyota and Nissan simultaneously. Since that year strict import controls have aided development although certain foreign cars— Austin, Renault, and Hillman—for many years were assembled locally.

The shipyards furnish another example of the "tool" industry. Since 1956 Japan has led the world in ship construction; in 1975 its yards launched approximately 15.2 million tons, 50 percent of the world tonnage. The industry's first launching way was constructed at Nagasaki as early as 1861; the Mitsubishi Company, aided at the beginning by generous government subsidies, soon took the lead and has maintained it to the present. World War II caused great damage to the Japanese shipyards and, until 1949, the tonnage completed annually was restricted by order of the Allied Occupation authorities. By 1952, however, the Korean War and later the closing of the Suez Canal stimulated the demand for big ships. Competition was keen because of the high cost of Japanese steel, and to this day there is intense rivalry between foreign and Japanese shipyards.

The Japanese have adopted many ways of revolutionizing shipbuilding, the most spectacular of which is the technique of block assembly. Entire sections of a ship are first made and assembled, sometimes in relatively distant factories, then brought to the launching way and welded there. This technique has reduced labor by one-third and the amount of metal used by 15 percent. More-over, a big ship of heavy tonnage can be built in two or three months less time than in an ordinary shipyard. These advantages, added to the substantial credit facil-ities allowed, have kept Japanese shipyards very busy, and 70 percent of the production today is destined for export. All shipbuilding is situated in the industrial belt, between Tokyo Bay (Tokyo, Kawasaki, Yokohama, Uraga, Yokosuka) and Sasebo and Nagasaki (where the huge Mitsubishi shipyards are located). There are more than 25 launching ways, with yards at Shimizu, Nagoya, Kobe, and, on the Inland Sea, at Aoi, In-noshima, Kure, and Shimonoseki. Nearby steel mills supply plates and beams. Half the ships exported are tankers; the rest for the most part are ore carriers, various types of freighters, and an increasing number of container ships.

Metal manufacturing, both light and medium, rep-resents 34 percent of Japanese industrial production. It is found either on the outskirts of an urban center or between metropolises. A shipyard is never located far from a populated center, while the automobile industry is generally established in the older parts of the megalop-olis. (The Nissan Company has its plants in and near Tokyo and the Toyota factories are located in Chukyo, near Nagoya.) Toyo Kogyo, the first company to pro-duce the rotary motor in Japan, is settled in Hiroshima. The machine tool and heavy electric appliance industries follow the same pattern; most of the factories (Fuji, Mi-tsubishi) are clustered around Osaka and Tokyo, with the outstanding exception of Hitachi, which was founded by private interests on the Pacific coast some 125 miles north of Tokyo and which builds the biggest turbines and generators in Japan.

The electrical appliance industry is even more systematically located. Since it depends upon labor, it is essentially an urban industry and therefore located in the Tokyo and Osaka areas. After 1955, with the rise in the standard of living, there was a rapid increase in domestic demand for such home appliances as television sets, heating and refrigerating units, washing machines, record players, and tape recorders. These articles, well made and relatively cheap because the work is done mostly by underpaid women, have become almost synonymous with Japanese exports. Their components— diodes, transistors, conductors, etc.—are manufactured in a number of small factories and then assembled in plants belonging to great companies like Matsushita and Sony, which are not only symbols but the most successful examples of the electrical appliance industry.

LIGHT INDUSTRY

The fourth group of Japanese industries takes in the light manufactures, also found mainly in the cities. Some of them—textiles, furniture, leather, printing—are quite ancient and over the years have developed a skilled labor force. The fact that their market is right at hand sets them apart from other industries. Here is found the largest number of small workshops, especially in the handicrafts, which are generally pursued as family businesses.

These workshops may have only one or two employees, often girls of around 16 who continue to work until the age of 22. They make every kind of article, many reminiscent of the past: fans, umbrellas, *geta* (wooden clogs), cushions, dolls, baskets, handmade paper, ceramics, and brocaded silks. These craftsmen sometimes form a community apart in a special quarter of the city, as in Kyoto's Nishijin, where a number of silk weavers have been established for a long time. Such craftsmen also manufacture accessories for the traditional Japanese house—tatami, *shoji* (moving partitions), wall plaster, and so on, while still others specialize in certain kinds of food.

Of all these manufactures, textiles are the most important because of the size of the mills and the financial structure of the industry, which place it midway between traditional handicrafts and modern industry. We have already mentioned the predominant role textiles played in the industrialization of the country; the industry still ranks second in the list of exports, and its total production in terms of value added is twice Great Britain's (but only one-third that of the United States or China). In the beginning, cotton and silk were the basic products, manufactured with raw materials from southern Kanto and the shores of the Inland Sea. In 1878 the Meiji government established a model spinning mill with the help of British experts. Thanks to an abundant supply of rural female labor, the industry grew rapidly; by 1934 Japan led the world in the manufacture of cotton piece goods, and textiles constituted 34 percent of its total industry and 70 percent of her exports. Today these figures are down to 8.5 and 19 percent, respectively.

The development of the textile industry has been interrupted or impeded several times. There was the silk crisis of 1931, the competition of synthetic materials after 1950, and the rivalry of countries with low standards of living and low wage scales like India and China. These two nations established their own textile industries comparatively late, but it was not long before they were flooding Japan's traditional markets in Asia and Africa with cheap merchandise. Japan countered by manufacturing and exporting textiles of quality such as silk, cotton, woolen, and synthetic piece goods. Nevertheless, Japan still must import all its wool and cotton, and while its productivity is superior to that of Great Britain, it is inferior to that of the United States.

Textiles are the most widely dispersed of the important Japanese industries. Cottons are made in the Inland Sea region, on the Nagoya and Kanto plains, and in the Toyama region in Hokuriku. Osaka and Nagoya have important mills, but there are few left in other parts of the country. The wool industry is relatively new and dependent upon Australian wool that is woven and spun in Nagoya, Osaka, and Yokohama. Japan still leads the world in the production of silk, but the quantity has declined by one-half since 1930 and today amounts to a mere 2 percent of total textile production (wool 11 percent, cotton 34 percent). Silk is produced and spun in south Kanto and Chubu but is woven in different and often distant places: Hokuriku, south Tohoku, and Kyoto, which specializes in the costly silks and sashes of the traditional kimono. Synthetic textiles amount to 35 percent of the total production and are manufactured everywhere, although the raw materials come from the big petrochemical centers described earlier. Synthetics are produced in east Tohoku, in Hokuriku, on Shikoku, on the mountains of Kansai, and on the borderlands of the Inland Sea (where the town of Kurashiki has the nation's largest rayon factories). Consequently, silk is no longer of importance, cotton and rayon seem to be losing ground, and the future of the Japanese textile industry appears to lie in wool and synthetics.

The Location of Japanese Industry

As we have seen, the principal industrial centers are found on the coasts or close to them. Even manufacturing zones that owe their existence to the two great coal-mining regions are on the coasts at points nearest to the mines. Muroran, for example, which is supplied by the Yubari fields, and Kitakyushu, which depends upon Chikuho, are on the seacoast and not on the coalfields themselves. The great metropolises of Tokyo, Osaka, and Nagoya, which furnish the capital and the directives, are also situated on the coasts; moreover, the industries themselves depend almost entirely for their raw materials and export trade upon the outside world that is accessible mainly by sea. Nevertheless, only a small fraction of the archipelago's 18,000 miles of coastline has been taken over by industry in the past century. Two-thirds of all production is still concentrated in the 350 miles that separate Tokyo Bay from Osaka Bay, and three-fifths of the remainder is scattered along the 275 miles between Osaka and the Straits of Shimonoseki.

This busy manufacturing belt, stretching 625 miles from the capital to Nagasaki, contains about 85 percent of all the economic activity of the country. The width of the belt varies, becoming broader on the plains of Kanto, Nagoya, and Osaka, and occasionally contracting until it disappears completely in the areas between Atami and Numazu on the Pacific or in several places on the Inland Sea. In this long and narrow ribbon of factories, worker cities, and market towns, there are

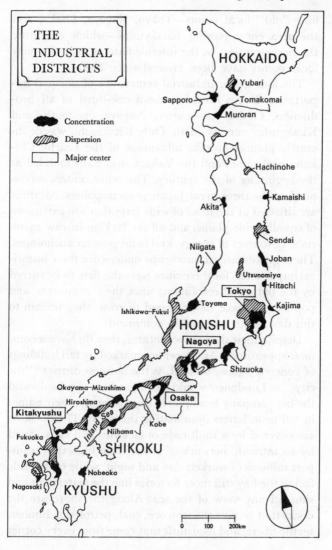

THE
INDUSTRIAL
DISTRICTS

HOKKAIDO

Yubari
Sapporo
Tomakomai
Muroran

Concentration

Dispersion

Major center

Hachinohe

Kamaishi

Akita

Sendai

Niigata

Joban

Utsunomiya
Hitachi
Tokyo
Kajima

Ishikawa-Fukui
Toyama

HONSHU

Nagoya

Shizuoka

Okayama-Mizushima
Hiroshima

Osaka

Kitakyushu
Kobe
Niihama

Fukuoka

Inland Sea

SHIKOKU

Nobeoka

Nagasaki

KYUSHU

0   100   200km

four "old" focal points—Tokyo, Nagoya, Osaka, and the area encompassing Kitakyushu—which constitute the nerve centers; in the intermediate areas, a few new focal points have been created since 1945.

The four major industrial centers are of unequal importance. Tokyo furnishes about one-third of all production, Osaka one-quarter, Nagoya one-tenth, and Kitakyushu one-twentieth. Only Kitakyushu was deliberately planned to take advantage of the nearby Chikuho coal mines and the Yahata steel mills founded at the beginning of the century. The other centers correspond to the three great Japanese metropolises. All three are situated at the head of wide bays that are extensions of equally wide plains, and all are lacking in raw materials, in sources of energy, and in deep-water anchorages. These grave natural handicaps underscore their historical importance, for these cities were the first to be stirred by the industrial revolution; since their commerce and populations have never ceased to grow, they remain to this day in the lead and in command.

Despite their distinctive features, they do have a common appearance. At the center, marked by tall buildings of concrete, glass, or steel, is the business district ("the city," as Londoners would call it), where the banks and the big company headquarters are located—their names in tall neon letters illuminating the night. The outskirts are covered by a multitude of factories and crisscrossed by an intricate network of urban train lines that transport millions of workers day and night, while on the side facing the bay still more factories line the waterfront and shut off any view of the sea. Along the shore are the docks that receive the iron ore, coal, petroleum, lumber, textile fibers, and foodstuffs that come from every corner of the nation and the world; in the shops, articles of every description are offered in increasing quantities and quality to vast numbers of consumers. Here, truly, is the heart of the nation's economic life.

Each sector, however, has a character of its own. The Hanshin (Osaka–Kobe) region was the first to be industrialized because it was the home, in 1868, of an enterprising group of wealthy merchants. Osaka's industry is an example of the second phase of Japanese industrialization; here a still important textile industry flourishes alongside an already significant heavy metal industry. Heavy machinery, shipyards, machine tools, and rolling stock head the list, but every branch of industry is represented, including heavy chemicals, light manufactures, and a complete line of household goods. Textiles, while still important, cannot be ranked with those of the Nagoya area, which remains the principal producer of wool, cotton, and artificial and synthetic fibers. Nagoya also furnishes a wide variety of products, from Toyota automobiles to the synthetic products of the petrochemical plants at Yokkaichi and Tsu on Ise Bay.

Tokyo Bay, embracing the older settlements of Tokyo, Kawasaki, Yokohama, and the recently reclaimed land on the shoreline to the north and in Chiba to the east, remains the most formidable industrial center of the archipelago. Here are located the largest labor pool and consumer market in the nation, and here, since the war, have been concentrated most of the official and private efforts to develop every type of manufacturing. These efforts are more "modern" than in the Osaka region and are characteristic of the third industrial period, marked by the near-disappearance of textile mills and the position of electrical appliances, shipyards, motor-cars, precision instruments, and plastics as the leading manufactures.

Over 600 miles separate Tokyo from the fourth established center of Japanese industry: Kitakyushu, on the Straits of Shimonoseki, and the adjacent metropolitan area of Fukuoka. Kitakyushu, whose share of total production is only five percent, trails far behind the other regions. It has the disadvantages of being situated a great distance from the other major metropolitan centers and of lacking room for industrial expansion; but above all it suffers from being located in a coal-mining region in the age of petroleum. For these reasons it has attracted fewer investments than the other three regions and is progressing far less rapidly today than the Inland Sea belt that separates it from Osaka Bay.

Major industries since 1950 have found room to develop in the areas that lie between these four conurbations. Already the borderlands of the Inland Sea produce more than ten percent of Japanese manufactures, especially the shore on the Honshu side. Here are the steel mills of Himeji and Mizushima; the petrochemical plants of Himeji, Aoi, Tokuyama, and Iwakuni; the carbochemicals of Ube; the shipyards of Aoi and Kure; and the automobile plants of Hiroshima. Along the Tokai, between Nagoya and Tokyo, chimneys and cracking towers line the waterfronts of Hamamatsu, Shizuoka–Shimizu, and Mishima–Numazu.

The 15 percent of industrial production that does not originate in the Fukuoka–Tokyo belt is scattered throughout the country. It is made up from large regional capitals and city-factories like the paper-mill towns of Ebetsu and Tomakomai and the steel mills of Muroran in Hokkaido; in Tohoku, it comes from the light industries at Sendai, the petrochemical and metallurgical complex at Hachinohe, the steel mills of Kamaishi, the heavy electrical machine factory at Hitachi, and the cluster of chemical plants around Utsunomiya and on the Joban coal fields. Akita and Niigata have refineries standing on their own oil fields; further south in Hokuriku, Takaoka and Toyama are other homes of heavy industry. Central Honshu has only the silk centers of the Kofu–Nagano region. Kyushu has some large chemical factories standing by themselves at Nobeoka, Oita, and near Omuta on the coal fields of Miike.

Generally speaking, however, the spectacular development of Japanese industry since 1952 has been restricted almost exclusively to the Tokyo–Fukuoka belt, as is evident from the regional increases in labor population since that year. Eleven of the 13 prefectures where the labor figures have risen faster than the average for the nation lie within the Kanto, Tokai, and Kansai regions. Taking 1955 at 100, in 1960 the Kanto average was 170.3, Kansai 154.6, and Chukyo (Nagoya) 151.9. This concentration was considered excessive and plans were made to decentralize in order to favor the poorer regions of north Kyushu, the Japan Sea littoral, south Kyushu, and Shikoku. In 1960 the General Planning Board proposed measures that would curtail investments in the three metropolises, divide the archipelago into economic spheres for better control of regional development, and encourage investment in south Tohoku, the interior of Kanto, north Kansai, Hokuriku, and the southern regions of Shikoku and Kyushu.

These measures are only beginning to be implemented. In the meantime, 95 percent of all investments are still made in the manufacturing belt, and the flow seems irrresistible, as existing installations attract new enterprises. However, within this industrial belt certain tendencies are already apparent. The most obvious is a general shift to the northeast. The percentage tables for the four great industrial regions for the years 1935 and 1960 clearly indicate a decline in the westernmost complex, Kitakyushu, an appreciable loss in Hanshin, a definite increase in Chukyo, and a real boom in the Tokyo region. Moreover, the fever to invest and to build huge installations, which for fifteen years has favored the Inland Sea basin, had spread by 1965 to the shores of Tokai and, more recently, to those of southern Tohoku on the Pacific side. The development of the Joban coalfields, the important heavy industry center at Hitachi, the founding in 1964 of a vast steel and petrochemical base at Kashima, the development of Sendai, and the gradual improvements at Hachinohe are ample evidence that the Japanese industrial belt is rapidly spreading along the Pacific coast north of the capital.

Thus we find the geography of industrial Japan represented (except for a few scattered centers) by a long, relatively narrow ribbon of factories that have their maximum concentration between Tokyo and Osaka but that also show considerable density between Osaka and the Straits of Shimonoseki. In the opposite direction, there is a rapidly developing strip between Tokyo and Tsugaru Straits, with Tomakomai, Muroran, and Sapporo as the northern terminals. This narrow band presents a striking contrast to the mountainous interior and the Japan Sea coast—areas which continue to remain rural and are the traditional sources of workers. It is this distribution of industrial activity that gives each region of the archipelago its distinct character.

Communications :
Internal and External

ALTHOUGH industry is heavily concentrated in a relatively small area of the archipelago, it is obvious that the Japanese have spread their activities over considerable distances. There are about 625 miles from Sapporo to Tokyo, 325 more to Osaka, and yet another 325 to Fukuoka. In the industrial and urban zones alone there are 625 miles in a direct line from the capital to the Straits of Shimonoseki, equal to the distance between New York and Detroit and, in just the Tokyo–Osaka sector, about the same number of miles as from New York to Pittsburgh.

Internal Communications

Domestic commerce is not hampered by these great distances. The important consumer markets are situated within the narrow belt extending from Tokyo to Fukuoka, but the basic commodities are drawn from widely scattered areas. Rice grows especially in Hokkaido, Tohoku, and north and northeastern Hokuriku; dairy products come from Hokkaido, meat from Chugoku and

185

Kyushu, wood from Hokkaido and Chubu, while coal is mined in the extreme north in Hokkaido as well as in southwestern Kyushu. Inversely, the growing domestic consumer market has led to an active trade between the areas manufacturing articles of everyday use such as clothing, tools, and electrical appliances—that is to say, the four industrial metropolises and the areas of the interior and the Japan Sea. In this case commerce is diffuse and uses the highways. Raw materials and food products, however, are generally transported by railroad or coastal ships.

Another feature of this domestic commerce is the location of industry and the metropolises which, with the exception of Kyoto, are on or near the coast. Transportation consequently is peripheral, since the mountains in the interior hinder communications. The insular character of the country makes coastwise transportation a necessity, while the great quantity of overseas trade concentrates an immense amount of commercial traffic in the ports.

THE TRANSPORTATION NETWORK—RAILWAYS

The railway network best illustrates these conditions. The first line, built in 1872, connected Tokyo and Yokohama and by 1887 had reached Osaka. Later the inland cities and those on the Japan Sea coast were also joined by rail, thanks to some remarkable feats of engineering. Of the 17,500 miles of railway, 650 miles are tunneled and again as many spanned by bridges and viaducts. Because the main lines follow the coast, they must cross a great many rivers at their widest points, near the mouths, while the branch lines must climb steep grades and pass through long and tortuous tunnels before they traverse the central mountain ranges. On the 200-mile Tokyo–Niigata line, which ten express trains cover daily in four hours, Mt. Mikuni is crossed near its summit by a tunnel 8 miles long that terminates in spiral tunnels at each end. Elsewhere landslides, sudden rises in the water level of rivers, and prolonged winters with their heavy snowfalls are responsible for a greater number of engineering problems than can be found in any Western country and make the Japanese railway network resemble that of the European Alps.

The railroad serves the interior of the country better than do the roads; the density of the rail network, 12.25 miles per square mile, is the same as that of France or Italy although inferior to that of Great Britain or the Benelux. Except on the New Tokaido Line, tracks throughout are narrow gauge because of the financial difficulties the system encountered in the beginning. The infrastructure was well built (heavy rails were used), and on the plains the trains travel at 70 miles an hour. Intensive use is made of the railways in Japan. Not only do the Japanese enjoy traveling from one end of their elongated country to the other, but the fast-growing metropolises have developed an enormous commuter traffic. Almost 112 billion passenger-miles are recorded annually (4 per railway mile), by far the highest figure in the world for passenger travel. Fifteen percent of the lines are double-tracked, and since electrification and the use of diesels are increasing rapidly, the last steam locomotives are being retired on the local lines.

Broadly speaking, the railroad follows both coastlines, beginning at Aomori in northern Honshu (where a ferry service ties it into the Hokkaido network) and running the length of the Pacific and Japan Sea coasts as far as

Lake Biwa, where the two main lines meet. They continue side by side as far as Osaka, where they separate once
again, one branch keeping to the shores of the Inland
Sea. At Shimonoseki they join once more and cross over
to Kyushu by an underwater tunnel. Like Hokkaido,
Shikoku has an independent network. The two trunk
lines on Honshu are connected by a number of transverse
lines that serve the interior of the country. These branch
lines are managed either by the National Railways,
which owns one-fourth of the entire network, or by local
private companies.

The railways handle about 14 percent of all domestic
freight. Coal is 25 percent of the tonnage, lumber 7 percent, cement 6 percent, followed by petroleum and its
by-products, minerals and metal products, and finally
rice. This freight is unequally distributed through the
nation. The Tokaido Line (Tokyo–Nagoya–Osaka) takes
care of 27 percent of the passenger traffic within a sector
representing only 2.4 percent of the total mileage. About
100 passenger trains and 60 freight trains travel over this
sector daily. Traffic doubled in 1964 after the construction of the New Tokaido Line with a "normal" gauge
(1.445 meters) and without sharp curves, and express
trains now make the run from Tokyo to Fukuoka in six
hours and fifty minutes. At night, fast freight trains use
the new line. Barely three years after it had opened, it
carried its one hundred millionth passenger. The Sanyo
Line is an extension of the Tokaido Line from Osaka to
Shimonoseki and is next in importance. The Hokuriku
and San-in lines handle mostly passengers, and even on
the national lines passenger traffic is slightly heavier
than freight, a situation opposite to the one that exists in
the United States, for example.

HIGHWAYS

Transportation by road was in its infancy until the early 1960s. This supplementary service, performed by trucks and buses in the United States, was hardly known in Japan because the roads lagged far behind the railroads, which, as in other industrial countries, preceded the automobile by a good half-century. In the feudal period five great highways which anticipated the roads of today connected Edo, the administrative capital of the nation, with the main sections of the country. The Tokaido road, which went as far as Kyoto and Osaka, was the most important, and the famous woodblock prints by Hokusai and Hiroshige depict the relay stations and the numerous travelers, the monks, pilgrims, merchants, and officials who passed along the road on horseback or on foot.

The automobile was a late arrival because of the difficult conditions that prevailed in the early years of Japan's modern economy. The roads suffered severely from the delay. Of the 18,750 miles of national highways, only one-quarter are wide enough to provide two lanes; although well maintained as a rule, barely two-fifths have an asphalt or cement surface. There are 95,000 miles of prefectural roads, 90 percent of them practicable for automobiles, but not over 12 percent are paved. Since 1960 an increasing percentage of the national budget has been assigned to road building and plans have been made for a network of expressways to connect all the major cities. The 325-mile highway joining Tokyo and Osaka was the first to be finished in 1969. The north and northeast, on the other hand, are still very far behind.

The disparities that are evident in the railway network exist also in the road system. The Pacific coast between

Tokyo and Osaka and the north shore of the Inland Sea
are the areas with the heaviest traffic. This is particularly true of trucks. Japan had about 10 million trucks
in 1975, and these have taken the lead over the railroads, especially on short and average-distance hauls,
with 82.8 million ton-miles (as against 33 million for
the railroads). Interurban bus lines are handling more
commuter travel, obliging some of the branch railway lines to suspend service. Including privately owned
automobiles, the total of motorized vehicles on the roads
of Japan was close to 28 million in 1975. Since these
roads are multiplying far less rapidly than are automobiles, traffic congestion is serious, and Japan today has
the highest accident rate per vehicle in the world.

AIRWAYS

Only the airlines are able to avoid the obstacles that
the country's topography has put in the way of roads and
railroads. Several airlines link the two great centers of
the country, Tokyo and Osaka, with most of the other
cities by at least one flight daily; for certain well-traveled
routes like Tokyo–Osaka, Osaka–Fukuoka, or Tokyo–
Sapporo, as many as ten round trips a day as well as night
flights at reduced rates are scheduled. The plane fares
are lower than those in Europe; the Tokyo–Sapporo
flight of 625 miles, for example, costs 30 percent less than
the Paris–Marseilles one of 415 miles. About 25 million
Japanese, or 2 out of every 9, traveled by plane in
1975. The New Tokaido railway line covers the distance
from Tokyo to Osaka in a little over three hours, which is
about equal to the flight time if one hour is added at each
end for transportation from airport to city center; nevertheless, the two cities are of such importance that both

means of travel are always booked beyond their capacities. For greater distances, on the other hand, flying is from 4 hours (Tokyo–Fukuoka) to 17 hours (Tokyo–Sapporo) faster, and the airlines are always busy. On the Tokyo–Sapporo run alone close to 4,000 seats are available each day (compared with 1,000 on the Paris–Lyons run). A quasi-government company, known by its English name of Japan Air Lines, and several private companies share this traffic. JAL also has an international service that covers most of the globe.

SEAWAYS

Transportation by sea has always been important in Japan, and to this day its low cost makes it one of the main channels of domestic commerce. The fact also that 65 percent of Japanese industry and 35 percent of the population are situated on the coast adds considerably to the traffic. Coastwise ships transport more than double the amount of tonnage carried by Japanese freighters in international trade. Roughly 51 percent of all merchandise shipped from one part of the archipelago to another travels by sea, whereas only 14 percent goes by rail and 35 percent by road. Sea traffic consists largely of goods shipped in bulk, of minerals, coal, lumber, and paper pulp transported from the point of origin, especially Hokkaido and north Kyushu, to the manufacturing centers of Honshu. Coal and coke constitute about one-half of the freight; then come the building materials (sand, stone, cement), metal and iron sands, and timber. Nearly 1,000 ports are served by this coastwise traffic which, in 1970, amounted to 120 billion ton-miles.

A large part of this maritime commerce is centered in the great metropolitan and manufacturing areas around

Tokyo, Nagoya, and Osaka bays and the Straits of Shimonoseki. Although on a more modest scale, the Inland
Sea has a considerable traffic in manufactured goods
destined particularly for Shikoku and is crisscrossed by
numerous ferries transporting travelers from one shore to
the other or serving the multitude of smaller islands.
Some of the coastwise traffic is handled by ocean-going
ships that call at several domestic ports before heading
overseas. However, unlike the overseas traffic in which
foreign ships have the greater share, the coastwise trade
is served exclusively by Japanese cargo vessels, sometimes of very limited tonnage.

International Exchanges

Japan's share of worldwide trade amounts to about
5 percent. This was already its portion before World
War II, although it has since doubled in real earnings
(for 1975: exports, $55 billion; imports, $60 billion). In
Chapter 1 were given the reasons trade became necessary
as soon as the country adopted a modern economy: a
lack of raw materials for its industry and food for its population on the one hand, and the need to sell its manufactured goods on the other. However, since World War
II a trend of great significance has been the development
of a domestic consumer market that is capable of absorbing an increasingly large share of this production. Nevertheless, trade with the rest of the world will continue to be
of paramount importance to Japan because about 15
percent of its production is exported, representing 14
percent of the national income. According to official
estimates, production will continue to increase at a pace
that will not only satisfy domestic demand but may also

stimulate exports to the point that by 1985 Japan will be the leading commercial nation of the world.

While growing substantially in volume, the nature of this commerce has changed greatly. In the nineteenth century, the need to import almost all of its raw materials and part of its foodstuffs forced the country to accept the "unequal treaties" that regulated its commerce with foreign nations until 1895. Japan in those days sold raw silk, tea, a superior quality of rice, cotton, and even coal. The silk shipments steadily increased until by 1914 they constituted one-half of all exports. Silk piece goods and the new cotton industry together represented 65 percent of all textile sales in 1929. The worldwide crisis of that year seriously affected the silk market, and metallurgical products began to assume a place in Japanese foreign trade. Since 1945 the substitution of metals for textiles has progressed steadily. From 52 percent before World War II, textiles dropped to 19 percent in 1965 and to 6.7 percent in 1975, while metals climbed to 64 percent in 1969. Machinery alone climbed from 3.6 to 38.9 percent between 1935 and 1973.

Imports of food products followed a similar pattern. These imports were indispensable at first, but the government sought to limit the volume by making the country self-sufficient. We have already mentioned the impetus this gave to Japanese agriculture. Since the 1960s, however, the high prices of domestic agricultural products have reversed the trend, and the tendency today is to purchase abroad whatever cannot be grown economically at home. Imports of cereals other than rice went from 2 to 9 million tons between 1960 and 1970, those of soybeans from 760,000 to 3 million tons. In parallel, the growing industrial production calls for increasing quantities of raw materials, and the exports necessary to finance these purchases will also continue to increase.

This grave dependence on the world market is found even in Japan's tools of trade. Its merchant marine, the third largest in the world before World War II, was three-quarters destroyed in 1944–45. By 1961, however, Japan had rebuilt 7 million tons, which was more than it had owned in 1940. This rose to 38 million tons by 1975, officially placing Japan second among the maritime powers, behind Liberia. The ships themselves have improved: by 1969, 75 percent were less than ten years old; semicargo ships, so numerous before the war, had almost disappeared. Today the big ships of heavy tonnage, the tankers and the ore ships, are the mainstay of the merchant fleet. Container ships are also being built in great numbers. While both tonnage and revenue have increased, these ships carry only a fraction of the nation's commerce. Whereas before 1940 the profits from using the Japanese fleet were twice the cost of using foreign carriers, today's recourse to the latter makes heavy inroads upon the country's foreign exchange.

THE IMPORTS

The list of Japanese imports in 1975 needs little comment: raw materials compose 63 percent of the total. Japan imports 100 percent of its cotton, wool, bauxite, nickel, and rubber; 99 percent of its ferrous metals and petroleum; 90 percent of its copper; 80 percent of its salt; 70 percent of its coal. Of food products, 80 percent of the wheat, 40 percent of the barley, and 60 percent of the soybeans are also imported. Combustible minerals (coal and petroleum), represent 20 percent of all purchases; raw materials 39 percent (textiles 11 percent, raw metallurgical products such as ferrous minerals, scrap iron, nonferrous metals 12 percent); food products 17 percent (including 2.4 percent for wheat). Manufactured goods amount to less than one-quarter of the total (23 percent), of which one-half is for tools and machinery and 5 percent for pharmaceutical and chemical products.

Before the outbreak of war in China in 1937, 10 percent of the purchases (one-half of the imports of iron, coal, and soybeans) were made in that country, which in return took 43 percent of the Japanese exports (including one-half of all cotton textiles). Since the war, the political situation and China's reluctance, until 1972, to buy the sophisticated products Japan now manufactures have reduced this trade to a negligible figure. The United States has supplanted China, furnishing about one-quarter of all Japanese imports—namely, most of the cotton, wheat, synthetic rubber, coke, and scrap iron. Australia is the next most important source of raw materials (wool, coal, iron, wheat, sugar). From Asia come the iron (Indonesia, Malaysia), the natural rubber (Malaysia), the petroleum (Middle East), and the timber. Latin America supplies sugar (Cuba), coffee (Brazil), and cotton (Mexico); Europe (West Germany and Great Britain in particular) supplies the machine tools.

Japan became a member of GATT (General Agreement on Tariffs and Trade) in 1955 in the hope of buying raw materials at better prices and finding new markets for its products in foreign countries. Beginning in 1960 it pursued this policy further by lifting some of its import restrictions. This policy was begun somewhat hesitantly because, age-old insular prejudices aside, many of Japan's manufactures were still not competitive. Automobiles, machine tools, petrochemicals, and especially agricultural products were more expensive than similar foreign items (with the one exception of mandarin oranges). In 1961 Japan's chief imports of wool, cotton, ferrous minerals, and paper pulp were exempted from customs duties. Also exempted were certain manufactured goods (cameras, radios, bicycles) that obviously could not compete in the Japanese market. By 1964, 93 percent of Japanese purchases abroad, including iron and steel, chemical products, and textiles, were entering free of duty. The consequences were felt at once, but a rapid, intense effort to modernize production, in the steel and automobile industries particularly, quickly checked the adverse effect and reversed the dangerous trend. For textiles, however, the contrary has been true. Japanese piece goods are unable to compete with those of India and China, and this in part explains their gradual disappearance from the list of Japanese exports.

Food products are the big problem. We have noted that their prices are always higher than those abroad. The question is whether Japan is prepared to stop subsidizing the farmer who grows 73 percent of the country's food or whether it should continue to invest in industry that gives employment to the excess rural population and thus pays for food imports. Countries like West Germany and the United States, which are members of GATT, protect their agriculture but not their industries, while Great Britain does the reverse.

THE EXPORTS

Japan's exports are those of an industrial country with two very different foreign markets. Among its customers are some highly industrialized nations who buy such sophisticated products as ships, radios and transistors, clothes, toys, electronic and photographic appliances, and machine tools. In that market, Japan still has an advantage because of its slightly lower wage scale and particular industrial structure. To less-developed countries Japan sells manufactured goods, but these are articles produced cheaply and in quantity like automobiles and bicycles, fertilizers, rails, machinery for clearing forests and for public works, steel bars, aluminum, and various chemical products. Taken together, machinery is 38.9 percent of total exports, metals 18 percent, and textiles 8.9 percent. More specifically, steel constitutes 13.2 percent of the sales, ships 8.4 percent, automobiles 5.5 percent, radio and television sets 3.2 percent.

One-third of all the exports go to the United States. Among these, one-quarter consists of textiles (silks, cotton, clothing), the balance of machinery (radios, cameras, sewing machines, cars), articles of wood, toys, ceramic wares, and canned fish. Europe and Australia import a similar assortment, the latter buying more because of its proximity. Exports to Great Britain are also increasing, although that country's entry into the Common Market may change the character of the trade. Underdeveloped countries account for about 50 percent of Japanese sales, in particular the nations of southeast Asia, long familiar to Japanese commerce, and South Korea. Nevertheless this percentage, 46 percent in 1975, represents a sharp drop from 1954 when it was 76 percent. The fact is that these countries are short of foreign exchange, and the rice, cotton, wheat, and sugar they themselves have to offer, despite the low prices, are a glut in the world markets.

China, while keeping most of its markets closed to Japanese products, has become a serious competitor, in textiles especially but also in fertilizers, ceramic wares, and cement. In Asia or Africa, whenever Japan tries to sell an entire plant or build a dam, it encounters serious competition from the West. However, because of the war indemnities to Asian countries, paid largely in merchandise and public works, Japan has made many new contacts, technical as well as commercial. Its influence in the underdeveloped nations has not come simply from selling them manufactured goods; it was gained by providing technical assistance, by giving aid to the mining industries (iron in India and Malaysia, petroleum in the Middle East, copper in the Philippines), and by helping to establish hydroelectric stations or assisting in agricultural projects. Japanese prices are not as widely competitive as is commonly believed. Raw materials are expensive and bank rates on loans higher than in the West, while the steady rise in wages offsets any early advantage the country may have had over other industrial nations.

World War II is responsible for certain prejudices that the aggressive Japanese merchant of today exacerbates at times. Several countries have closed their markets to Japanese products to protect their infant industries, and also because the specter of an invasion—however pacific this time—still haunts some of their leaders. There is no doubt that Japan suffers because of this attitude, not only in the countries it invaded in 1937–45 but also among the more distant adversaries of those days, the big Western powers. Faced with these problems, Japanese businessmen have perfected some remarkable techniques for pursuing their commercial aims, among them the custom of prospecting in groups. Well-organized teams make a thorough survey for the marketing of a single article as efficiently as they gauge the future prospects of a country.

Of the three great powers that surround Japan—China, the USSR, and the United States—it is the most distant one with which the nation has the most trade. The United States is Japan's principal supplier as well as its best customer, a relationship that still greatly influences the political attitude toward this former adversary. Southeast Asia, an old business partner, is next. Western Europe takes third place, due mainly to the volume of trade with West Germany. Petroleum is the reason the Middle East assumes fourth place, although the area buys little in return. Africa, the most recent of Japan's customers, is growing so fast in commercial importance that the continent has already equaled the figures for Latin America, a client of long standing. Most remarkable is the still relative insignificance of exchanges with the two great neighboring powers, the USSR and China, who are responsible for a paltry 3 and 4.1 percent, respectively, of all Japanese trade.

Japanese-Soviet trade only amounted to about $2.8 billion in 1975. Of shipments from Japan to the Soviet Union, machinery accounted for 40.4 percent and textiles 22.6 percent. Ninety-five percent of Soviet exports to Japan were raw materials, of which timber accounted for 38 percent, cotton 12.7 percent, and coal 8 percent. A few private agreements, such as that of 1971 by which Mitsui Kogyo and Tokyo Kikai sold the Soviets four factories for the manufacture of synthetic products, are made each year. These exchanges, however, amount to only one-thirtieth of Japan's total commerce.

Some recent agreements have opened up the possibility of improved Japanese-USSR commercial relations, however. The projects now under negotiation between the two nations include those concerning the development of natural gas in Yakucha, oil in Tyumen, coking coal in southern Yakucha, forests in the Soviet Far East, and prospecting for oil and natural gas on the continental shelf off Sakhalin.

Until 1963, difficulties of a strictly political nature had obstructed trade with China and impeded a natural rapprochement between these two countries with obviously complementary economic resources. At the peace talks held in September 1972, China decided to normalize its relations with Japan and renounced its war reparations claim, which would have amounted to a tremendous sum.

A substantial part of Japan's trade with China is the barter of oil for steel. Japanese manufacturers of heavy industrial machinery are also concerned about the prospect of selling complete plants to China. Since the establishment of official relations in 1972, Japan has sold eight plants with a total value of about $800 million. But recent steel talks ended in a small figure because both sides could not agree on price and credit terms. Sino-Japanese trade in 1975 was $3.8 billion, on which China ran a deficit of $730 million. The 1974–76 recession contributed to a slowdown in the rate of increase of commercial relations between these two countries.

THE PORTS

Of the thousand or more ports that mark the coasts of Japan, only 68 are open to foreign shipping and most of the traffic is confined to about a dozen. Tokyo and Osaka acquired very early the deep-water ports of Yokohama and Kobe, and these two still head the statistical tables for annual traffic. However, very large port facilities are being constructed today on low-lying stretches of the coast, at the head of the bays that shelter the larger cities, and on land reclaimed for industrial use where new docks can now accommodate tankers, ore-carriers, and container ships. Of the limited number of deep-water ports, only Nagasaki and Kure are of major importance because they are situated in the industrial zone.

More than half the traffic is confined to the bays of Tokyo and Osaka, Tokyo Bay alone accounting for one-third (240 million tons in 1964, 320 million in 1970, and at least 450 million in 1975). Osaka is growing even more rapidly on the enormous polders the city built along the 32-mile front from Sakai to beyond Kobe (120 million tons in 1967 and 250 million in 1975). Ise Bay, wherein lie Nagoya and the industrial ports of Yokkaichi and Tsu, should reach 200 million tons before 1978. The advance of heavy industry—petrochemicals and steel—along the Pacific coast and the shores of the Inland Sea has multiplied the number of ports, each area preferring to take care of its own maritime traffic.

Statistically, Kobe and Yokohama between them handle 60 percent of Japan's imports and 40 percent of its exports. Following these come Nagoya, Osaka, and Tokyo, each one accounting for 8 percent of all foreign trade. These five ports together serve the three major industrial agglomerations and are responsible for four-fifths of the nation's imports and three-fifths of its exports. The imports consist mostly of heavy raw materials and the traffic in them is fairly well concentrated, whereas the exports, especially of manufactured goods, are shared by a large number of ports. In fact the traffic in these ports is but the maritime front of Japanese industry, and the location of this industry determines where the traffic will be concentrated.

Eleven Regions:
The Privileged and the Neglected

FOR ADMINISTRATIVE purposes, Japan is divided
into eight large regions or districts: Hokkaido, Tohoku,
Kanto, Chubu, Kansai (or Kinki), Chugoku, Shikoku,
and Kyushu. These districts in turn are divided into 47
prefectures (*ken*), which are the nation's major administrative divisions.

If we subdivide two of the largest of these regions,
Chubu and Chugoku, on the basis of their histories and
natural geographical divisions, we can talk about 11
regions that have existed in similar form (though different name) for centuries.

The history of Japan is a history in part of the movement of its people in a northeasterly direction through
the archipelago, beginning in Kyushu and moving toward Hokkaido; as it moved north, this migration formed
zones of varying density. During the late feudal period
(early seventeenth century), the country was divided
into large fiefs, often coextensive with natural regions.
This history gave each district its own distinctive character, which each has been able to maintain to some
extent over the years. Today regional variants are consid-

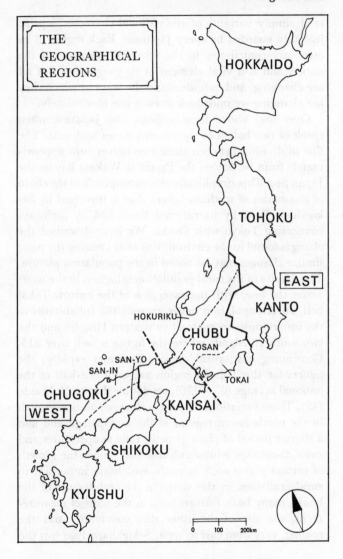

THE
GEOGRAPHICAL
REGIONS

HOKKAIDO

TOHOKU

EAST

KANTO

HOKURIKU

CHUBU

TOSAN

SAN-YO

SAN-IN

TOKAI

CHUGOKU

WEST

KANSAI

SHIKOKU

KYUSHU

0   100   200km

ered simply variants of the national character, a prize jealously guarded by every Japanese. Each region in its own way contributes to the economic progress of the nation and is a vital element of its geography. But all are changing, and to understand the ways in which they are changing we must look at each one more closely.

Over and above these regions, the Japanese often speak of two halves of the country—east and west. The line of division between these two halves runs approximately from Ise Bay on the Pacific to Wakasa Bay on the Japan Sea. Topographically this corresponds to the chain of mountains of medium height that is traversed by Sekigahara Pass, by its railroad lines, and by highways connecting Tokyo with Osaka. We have described the changes found in the environment after crossing the pass; similar changes may be noted in the population picture. The density of the rural population is highest in the west; across the line, with the exception of the narrow Tokai belt, rural population never exceeds 188 inhabitants to the square mile, in contrast to western Honshu and the two southern islands where the figure is well over 315. Continuing east, rural density decreases rapidly; the figures for the Tohoku region are only one-half of the national average (87 to 170), yet double that for Hokkaido (42). These variations indicate a slow population growth in the northeastern regions of the archipelago and also a shorter period of plant growth. Low temperatures and snow discourage winter cultures and hinder the growth of certain plants such as reeds, which are important to rural craftsmen in the west. In the architecture of the house, many basic features such as the units of measurement, the size of the inner dirt courtyard, and the roofing, vary from east to west. Sekigahara Pass was the

scene of a decisive battle in 1600, and its historic importance is explained by this division of the country into two
great zones, in each of which Japanese culture developed
differently: the west, composed of Kyushu, Shikoku, the
San-in and San-yo sections of Chugoku, and Kansai,
occupied from an early age and with a colorful history;
and the east, which includes the Hokuriku, Tosan, and
Tokai sectors of Chubu, Kanto, Tohoku, and, of course,
Hokkaido, settled and developed at a later date.

But an even more important line of demarcation is
one that cuts across the Sekigahara line and separates
the "inner" from the "outer" zone. This clearly divides
Japan longitudinally and gives it a "front" and a "back,"
human as well as geographical. We have already noted
the environmental differences, particularly in climate,
between these two halves of the islands in the winter.
Even greater is the contrast in population. The "outer"
zone contains the Pacific coast and the Inland Sea from
Tokyo Bay to the Straits of Shimonoseki. Most of the
population is concentrated here, with immigration constantly adding to the numbers. This coastal belt is composed of a succession of plains and quiet bodies of water
extending from Kyushu, the heart of prehistoric Japan,
through the Inland Sea, the Kansai corridor, Lake Biwa,
and across the plains of Tokai to Nagoya, Shizuoka, and
Kanto. It is the natural highway to the northeast that
men followed in search of new lands; as a consequence,
all the big cities as we know them today are found along
the way. The two capitals, first Kyoto, then Edo, as well
as the old commercial center of Osaka, were founded in
this manner, attracting men and capital from all parts
of the country. It was here, after 1868, that the economic
power of the nation was concentrated, the state and a

few powerful families working closely together during the early years of the Meiji Restoration. The dissimilarity between the "outer" and the "inner" zones has never ceased to grow. In 1873, Nagoya and Kanazawa, both former feudal capitals, the one on the Pacific or "outer" zone, the other on the Japan Sea, the "inner" zone, had nearly equal populations: 125,000 and 109,000, respectively. By 1898 there was already a pronounced difference—244,000 and 84,000; and the disparity increased through the years: 608,000 and 137,000 in 1920, 1.32 million and 201,000 in 1940, and in 1970, 3 million for the Nagoya conurbation and 300,000 for Kanazawa.

The Neglected Regions

What have been termed the forgotten regions of Japan could well include, in addition to San-in, Hokuriku, and most of Tohoku (all of them a part of the "inner" zone), southern Kyushu and Shikoku and northeastern Hokkaido. Each one of these regions has a distinctive character that derives from such features as climate, isolation, or local tradition rather than from any contribution to the economic life of the country. A severe climate is common to all these areas: bitter cold and long periods under snow in the north and northeast, typhoons and torrential rains in the south. But these vagaries of nature threaten the populated regions as well. (Kanto, for instance, has devastating earthquakes.) More serious is the isolation. The high mountains of southern Kyushu and Shikoku, the immense forests of central Honshu, the great distances—these shut out the influences of the great urban centers and preserve a way of life and work that belongs to the past. These regions cling to rural life and its traditional customs; since their people are very prolific, over the past century they have become an important source of manpower for the busier sectors of the country. Despite these limitations, they have succeeded in developing a few industrial and commercial areas of minor importance; these have never become real urban or manufacturing centers, however, because of their isolation.

First let's look at Tohoku, which occupies the northern third of Honshu. With an area of 41,800 square miles and a population of 10 million, it has the relatively low average of 87 inhabitants per square mile, living in three parallel corridors that are separated by high mountains. The terrain resembles the large plateau region of the French Massif Central, as do the old customs of the region and its sharp contrast of the highly contemporary alongside so many relics of the past. The irregular topography and a climate dominated by long winters are some of its harsher features. Agriculture is one chief activity and occupies every basin; immense areas are covered by rice fields. In the heights (Mt. Abukuma, Mt. Kitakami) that separate the valleys, animal husbandry is increasing. Fruit orchards are numerous in Yamagata and Fukushima in the south and Aomori in the far north. Near Akita, the recent reclamation of Hachirogata lagoon opened up more than 75 square miles to modern agriculture, and on Mt. Iwate close by, the slopes are occupied by cattle farms. Industry is scattered and depends upon local resources: metallurgy upon the Kamaishi iron ore mines, petrochemicals upon the Akita oil fields, coal upon the Joban basin. The region also contains about one-third of the Japanese hydroelectric reserves. Finally, the fishing industry has been successfully revived and exploited by large associations on the Pacific coast, at Shiogama and Ishinomaki in particular, and further north at Hachinohe. All this, however, does not add up to a progressive modern region, despite the growing significance of Sendai, the largest city in the province.

Hokuriku is a prolongation of the western flank of Tohoku, the wide plains and the precipitous coast extending south along the Japan Sea for over 300 miles. Beyond Wakasa Bay lies San-in, formed on a smaller scale and stretching to the Straits of Shimonoseki. This is the "inner" zone, covering 625 miles from north of Niigata to the approaches to Kitakyushu, and composed of a succession of distinctive and, until recently, backward regions. In Hokuriku proper, open plains terminate in low hills that form a stairway to the Hida Mountains. Here winter is the dominant feature and snows blanket the heights and depressions from December until early April. In the summer the rice fields cover the floor of the basins with a colorful carpet that slowly changes from green to yellow. This region is one of the granaries of Japan, an area of large farms, of houses clustered on alluvial ridges, as in Niigata, or dispersed over the plains, as in Toyama.

The San-in region does not give a similar impression of space, except near Yonago and Matsue. It is an area of small plains, mere exits to the valleys, and of promontories that have crumbled into the sea where they have formed little islands and reefs. On nearly every creek is a fishing village. Rice is almost the only culture. The winters here are also snowbound, and every farm seeks shelter from the blizzards behind a wall of tall trees. Tohoku, Hokuriku, and San-in are severely isolated from the great urban centers; their commercial needs have to be cared for by different cities, a situation that deprives them of a true focus and a sense of regional unity.

A third aspect of these neglected regions is found in the southernmost reaches of the archipelago, in Shikoku and Kyushu. The unifying element of this area is the climate, and summer is the dominant season. The most isolated area is the southern tip of Kyushu, where tall, massive mountains cut off the plains of Miyazaki, Kumamoto, and Kagoshima (the site of the city most distant from Tokyo, 930 miles by rail) from the vital areas of the island that are grouped in the northwest between Nagasaki and Kitakyushu. These irregular elevations, largely of volcanic origin (Mt. Kirishima, Mt. Aso), seriously hinder communications in central Kyushu (to travel from Fukuoka to Kagoshima takes four hours by express train). They rise out of a multitude of small plains planted in rice, the paddies ascending the nearest slopes in a succession of terraces. Many customs inherited from the old feudal land divisions (*Kyushu* means "the nine provinces"), many festivals, types of buildings, and family relationships are native to this central and southern part of the island. Despite their size, the cities of Kumamoto, Miyazaki, and Kagoshima, each with about 300,000 inhabitants, are little more than administrative and commercial centers, for the government has sought to develop industry in the two coastal areas of Hyuga–Nobeoka and Oita. A similar situation exists in the southern part of Shikoku, which is sheltered by a semicircle of forested and sparsely inhabited hills but open to the Pacific, whence come frequent and devastating typhoons. The old province of Tosa has more reason to complain of its isolation than of its climate, however, since the long, hot season and the heavy rains make it possible to harvest two crops a year.

Thus in every sector solid mountain barriers separate the neglected regions from the Japan of the cities. The barriers generally take the form of a continuous chain, as in Chugoku, Kansai, and Shikoku, but elsewhere they sometimes constitute distinctive and independent regions in themselves, as on the Kii Peninsula, for example, or the Tamba Mountains that embrace the Kansai plains, or again in Tohoku, between the long, narrow plains. Hokkaido furnishes a further example, but the best illustration is in central Honshu, at the widest part of the archipelago, where the Tosan range separates Hokuriku from Tokai. We have already described this region of massive mountains traversed by wide, elongated valleys that are marked by occasional depressions. The latter form just so many rural or urban islands, cut off from each other by strips of forested land. On almost every plain stands an important agglomeration, either of feudal origin like Matsumoto, Kamisuwa, Kofu, and Takayama, or of religious derivation like Nagano. The soil is well tended and grows fruit, mulberries, and rice, especially on the lower slopes of the hills. Higher up, as far as the tree line, are the wastelands. Nevertheless, the life and appearance of these plains are in no way different from those of other regions; it is the strictly mountainous sectors, rather, that are a world apart and that constitute the fourth type of terrain in these neglected regions of Japan.

As we observed in connection with agriculture, the Japanese farmer is constantly aware of the mountains around him. As we indicated earlier, of the approximately 12.5 million acres he cultivates, 2.3 million are on slopes with a grade of over 15 degrees. The mountains have wood and his traditional fuel, charcoal, supplied by the ubiquitous woodcutter and charcoal-burner. Many of the most rugged areas like Mt. Kitakami in Tohoku, Mt. Totsugawa on the Kii Peninsula, or the Tosan range, are the homes of farmers who have settled on the banks of streams or, more often, on the steep slopes, on narrow platforms dug out of the mountainside, or on the edge of leveled terraces. In Tohoku, the horse still does the work and supplies manure; elsewhere, labor is by hand. In the north and center, the land is worked only part time; men, women, and animals move into the mountains for the summer months, plant a crop which they harvest in the autumn, then return to the plains. In Tohoku, trappers (*matagi*) build snow huts each winter from which they hunt fox and other fur-bearing animals.

HOKKAIDO

From every point of view, Hokkaido seems a region apart. It is not one of the neglected regions, for it has a distinct and very modern economy, yet it cannot be included in the key regions that form a continuous chain from Tokyo Bay to the west. It is a land of bitter cold and deep snow that allows little time for anything to grow. As already noted, it was the last island of the archipelago to be settled. In many respects it can be said to stand midway between the neglected regions and the key areas.

Its capital, Sapporo, was founded in 1885 on a swamp. By 1889 the early settlers had reached the Okhotsk Sea, bringing their rice culture with them. A unique control of the environment is characteristic of the island, and its products and methods of work have given it a special, almost exotic reputation. The intense cold creates problems for the farm animals, so every farm has a stable and a silo, and horses are plentiful for hitching to the wagons in summer and sleighs in winter.

Besides a number of original farm products, Hokkaido is exceptionally rich in minerals. In the ground lie half of the Japanese coal deposits, 99 percent of the mercury, 100 percent of the chrome, 78 percent of the natural gas (approximately 1,000 billion cubic yards), 27 percent of the iron ore (iron sands especially), and 43 percent of the gold. Energy is plentiful and varied and Hokkaido has created both heavy (steel at Muroran) and light industries (paper at Tomakomai and Ebetsu, woodcraft, canned goods) which find a ready market in the rest of the country. From the urban south to the northeast where the frontier is advancing laboriously through the fogbound hills of the Konsen plateau, the island is unified and well served by an excellent railway system that connects the hinterland and the urban centers with Sapporo as the hub. When this metropolis is joined to Honshu by road and railroad as it will be when the undersea tunnel now under construction is completed in about 1980, Hokkaido's ties with the vital centers of the nation will be closer; it will however, never lose its unique character that derives from its climate, its resources, and the activities of its population.

The Key Regions

In contrast to the neglected regions of north, central, and south Japan, the key regions of the country form a continuous belt some 625 miles long that extends roughly from east-northeast to west-southwest in a straight line through Kanto, Tokai, Kansai, the Inland Sea, and north Kyushu. Thus situated, these regions share certain natural conditions: mild winters with little snow, similar vegetation, and above all, easy intercommunication. From Tokyo Bay, the belt stretches along the Pacific shores to the important hot-springs resort of Atami, then ascends to Hakone Pass. On the other side lies Suruga Bay; once past Numazu, Shizuoka, Hamamatsu, and Toyohashi, we come to the Nobi Plain and the Nagoya conurbation. Sekigahara Pass then leads into the Lake Biwa basin where the Kansai corridor begins. After passing through Kyoto and Osaka, the corridor opens out onto the Inland Sea with its many islands and small coastal plains. Leaving Kobe, Himeji, Okayama, and Hiroshima behind, we finally reach the Straits of Shimonoseki. This is the heart of the "outer" zone of Japan, and today, the concentration here of the great cities and national wealth has given these regions unrivaled power in the archipelago.

KANTO

Kanto is the most northerly region of the inner zone. With the possible exception of Hokkaido, few regions of Japan are so well integrated. This integration is first of all geographic. Most important is the Kanto Plain, the largest in Japan (2,700 square miles), open to the ocean on the southeast and bound on the north and west by a double crescent of hills and high mountains. Mt. Fuji rises 65 miles to the west of Tokyo; also visible from the capital are the volcanoes of Mt. Nantai and Mt. Nasu. To cross the mountain barrier the roads and railroad must burrow through tunnels or climb steep slopes, except to the north, where the Shirakawa corridor of tectonic origin opens a way to Tohoku. The Kanto region is, above all, the most thickly populated area of the country. The density, 282 to the square mile, is greater than in any other region. One out of every three Japanese lives in this region. The density is highest on the shores of Tokyo Bay, where the figure is 1,847 for the Tokyo area, 595 for Kanagawa Prefecture (wherein lies the city of Yokohama); population density decreases rapidly toward the periphery and is less than 19 in the most remote areas, close to the summits of the mountains.

Agriculture follows the concentric pattern suggested by the terrain. Life in the mountains is similar to that in other mountainous areas, but the influence of Tokyo is rapidly erasing any traces of the past. The forests are intensively exploited because of the enormous demand for lumber from the capital, thus generating work for many laborers. The need for hydroelectricity has led to the construction of a number of artificial lakes in the less-populated areas, and some of the water is used to irrigate the plains downstream. Today, 12 million city dwellers are turning these heights into a center for tourists, a resort area for the summer and winter holidays. To reach the hotels and hot springs, roads, railways, and ropeways have been built, and over the years richer Tokyoites have established their second homes here. Despite this invasion, the traditional ways of rural life have not completely disappeared. Here, particularly in the heights to the south and also in the Chubu basin (Nagano, Suwa), is the birthplace and home of Japanese sericulture, which for more than a century before its recent decline brought wealth to generations of farmers. This history is evident in the air of affluence of the big farmhouses, solidly erected on the edge of the terraces or on the slopes, with second-floor balconies reserved for raising silkworms. Elsewhere are mountain villages still faithful to an even more distant past, cultivating taro and a few cereals in ways and amid surroundings that closely resemble those of the Cevennes mountain range in southern France.

But the real agricultural effort is focused on the plains. The Tone River and its tributaries have worn wide channels that make it easy to irrigate the rice fields planted between their high embankments. The mulberry is found everywhere; the rest of the fields and terraces furnish such dry crops as wheat or barley for the breweries in the north. On the outskirts of Tokyo are the market gardens that grow flowers and vegetables under vinyl according to the most modern methods, but they are being forced to retreat as the urban pressure grows. The northern reaches of the province are colder and favor the cattle farms that furnish milk and meat. The plains extend for miles in every direction, forming an immense, flat expanse that is unique in Japan; the fields are dotted with villages, hamlets, or dispersed farms, each surrounded by a tall hedge of trees. Snow is seldom seen more than 12 days a year, but the winter monsoon is cold and dry and sweeps across the flatlands in icy gusts. The coast provides little shelter and is extremely irregular. Tokyo Bay has deep water and is embraced by the Boso and Miura peninsulas, on whose shores are located many busy fishing ports like Misaki on Miura and Choshi at the mouth of the Tone River. There are excellent fishing grounds offshore where the warm waters of the Kuroshio join the cold Oyashio current. A string of cities lies on the periphery of the plain, almost every one a thriving market town that has grown up at the entrance to a crowded valley. In addition to acting as centers where mountain products can be exchanged for those of the lowlands, these cities serve as suburban residential areas for the metropolitan agglomeration whose intensive industrialization has become a menace to them all.

TOKAI

West of Hakone Pass, at the foot of Mt. Fuji, lies Tokai. It is a region of irregular shores, small coastal plains, rocky capes, and long beaches that extend from the Izu Peninsula to the deep-water bay of Ise. Here two kinds of rural scenery alternate. One consists of plains planted in rice, turning to dry crops, generally wheat, in the winter and to market crops on the approaches to the cities. Sunshine is abundant even in the cold season, and vegetables and certain fruits, like the strawberries of Shizuoka, will grow even in the depths of winter. The other type of scenery is the often-terraced hills covered with orchards of persimmons and tangerines, and, on the gentler slopes, the corrugated tea plantations.

But the real importance of the Tokai lies in its relation to the adjacent regions. It was the highroad that connected the cities of Kansai, Osaka, and Kyoto with the north and with Edo in particular. The Tokaido road used to thread its way through the region under a cover of ancient pines, wandering through steep passes and crossing many rivers. When Edo changed its name to Tokyo in 1868 and the industrialization of Osaka, Nagoya, and Tokyo began, the first railway and the first modern road were built in order to connect these cities; these were followed, after the Second World War, by the Shinkansen (the bullet train) and an express highway. Rapid communications stimulated commerce, and immigrants arrived in great numbers. Today the population density of Tokai is about 232 to the square mile, thus extending almost to Kansai the high population figures and intensive activity of Kanto.

KANSAI

After Kanto, Kansai is the most prosperous region of Japan. It has a special character which it owes as much to history as to geography. This is the historic center of the Japanese nation and the site of all its former capitals, including Nara and Kyoto; from these small plains the founders of the nation set out to conquer the northern half of the archipelago and civilize the whole country. Here for ten centuries the brilliant Kyoto court and, after 1700, the wealthy merchants of Osaka fostered and developed a national culture. Geographically Kansai is exceptionally well situated. It borders on three seas: the Japan Sea to the north, the Pacific to the south, and the Inland Sea; its hinterland contains a succession of fault basins that form a continuous corridor from the foot of Sekigahara Pass to the Inland Sea. Two great ranges protect this depression, Mt. Tamba to the north and the mountains of the Kii Peninsula to the south. There are striking differences in climate between the central plain, with its rather continental temperatures, and the two great upland areas that embrace it. The Tamba Mountains are blanketed by the snows of the winter monsoon while the Kii Range enjoys a very mild climate, except for the southwest slopes that belong to tropical Japan.

This contrast between the corridor and the mountains that enclose it has shaped the human geography of the province. The steep, forbidding character of the north and south ranges has forced all lines of communication between west Japan and the northeast to be channeled through the short corridor that leads from Lake Biwa to Osaka Bay. The two principal railroad lines and the main roads of north Honshu, after following the shores of the Pacific and the Japan Sea, meet here to form a single strand; once past Kyoto and Osaka it unravels and divides again. Osaka is the northern terminal of the shipping lines that serve the Inland Sea and connect with Shikoku and Kyushu.

This heavy concentration of urban life and lines of communication in the plains has intensified the isolation of the two adjacent ranges. Sparsely inhabited, almost inaccessible by railway, and still heavily forested, these mountains support a primitive sort of rural life very similar to the life of the mountain people of the neglected regions. Age-old customs are still practiced, and houses, in architecture and materials used, show evidence of old skills that the plains have long since forgotten. The great Buddhist sanctuaries of Hasedera, Muroji, and others, found near the ancient capitals, have made these lonely valleys familiar to city dwellers, and tourism to this day continues to contribute substantially to their prosperity. Nevertheless, the ancient crafts of weaving and wood-carving, the ceramics of Tamba, the few crops grown especially for the cities nearby—all of these have not been enough to stem the flow of the population to the plains.

Seen from those lonely heights, the plains appear to be forever wrapped in mist yet intensely active. On the 40-odd miles between Otsu on Lake Biwa and Osaka, roads and railroads, factories of every description, and towns of all sizes are gradually replacing the rice paddies. Agriculture has stayed alive by specializing either in market garden produce or in the teaplant which, in this district, boasts a famous brand known as Uji. Here on the Yamato Plain, Nara flourished in the seventh century, only to revert to rice fields after Kyoto was founded. Today it has repossessed the site. On the plain that is crisscrossed by canals and embankments, here and there still appears a large village bordered by an old moat. As a vestige of an earlier age, only an occasional handsome farmhouse still remains, its high mud walls hiding everything but the thatch roof and the outbuildings. Elsewhere, the fields with their vinyl stripes and the long, low buildings housing the chicken farms indicate the presence of a city not far away. Here more than in any other region, a past preserved with difficulty and a present eagerly welcomed are found side by side, at times even overlapping.

SAN-YO

The area on the Inland Sea's north shore that begins at Osaka and is a western prolongation of the Kansai plain has always been favored because it is the direct route between the Osaka conurbation and the Straits of Shimonoseki; anything traveling via the Shikoku shore must be transshipped. *San-yo* means "slope facing the sun," and its ribbon of plains and promontories has been, through the centuries, the highroad from Kyushu to Kansai. Like Tokai, the primary use of these borderlands is as a thoroughfare for the roads and railroads that join the cities of Kansai to Kitakyushu and Fukuoka. Communication here is not as easy as between Tokyo and Nagoya, and bridges and tunnels are numerous, especially between Okayama and Hiroshima. On the long irregular coast are many small peninsulas of granite rock capped by pines; in the misty atmosphere that generally prevails, they give a very Japanese effect to the scene.

As in Tokai, the southern exposure is responsible for the growth of a number of large urban centers. Climate and geography encouraged people from ancient times to settle in this region; it was not long before the feudal capitals of Himeji, Okayama, and Hiroshima were flourishing and acquiring active lives of their own.

Even the sea is densely populated. It is studded with islands and traveled by ships of every size and description that serve the many scattered settlements. The mountains of Chugoku and Shikoku shelter it from the winds of the Pacific and the Japan Sea, which from the beginning have been the great highway between Kyushu and Kansai. In Chapter 1 were described the busy economic life of these shores and the historic function of the farmer, the fisherman, and the artisan who supported the large population and prepared it for the industry and urban life of today.

That life and that industry have existed for a long time on the Straits of Shimonoseki where the crowded highroad terminates. Across the water from the old merchant city and fishing port of Shimonoseki are the coalfields of Chikuho and, 30 miles beyond, the feudal capital of Fukuoka, together forming a vast urban and manufacturing region that extends, not always uniformly, all the way to Nagasaki, Sasebo, Ariake Bay, and the coalfields of Miike. In contrast to the south and east shores of Kyushu, which are shut in by high mountains, the northwestern coast is seriously eroded and open to the sea. For centuries this stretch of the coast has been in touch with the world outside; here, long ago, Japanese sailors and merchants embarked to trade with the Philippines and other nations of southeast Asia, and to these same shores came the first Westerners—the Portuguese, Spanish, and English—and the Chinese to establish their trading posts. In still earlier times this northwest corner of Kyushu was the bridge to China. Monks, official delegates, and merchants arriving in Japan from Pusan in Korea landed at Hakata (now Fukuoka), then traveled to Kansai by the easy Inland Sea route. Until the Meiji Restoration of 1868, this was Japan's gateway to the outside world. The end of the nineteenth century saw the traffic reversed. The imperial road leading from Tokyo and Osaka to the rich colonies of Korea and North China left Japan at Fukuoka or Nagasaki, touched at Pusan, continued overland to Seoul and Pyongyang, then crossed the Yalu River to Dairen and the rich plains of Manchuria before disappearing into North China.

There is, as we have seen, a great contrast between the backward regions of the archipelago that face either the open sea or the frozen solitude of the north and those regions that lay in the historic path of national development and therefore acquired a concentration of population and wealth that has never ceased to grow. Although nature contributed in large measure to this partition— providing an inhospitable coast and long and snowbound winters on one side, and on the other the wide plains, favorable exposures, and safe anchorages—until recent times the choice of settlement (an unconscious choice, it is true) was left to man. To fix upon this plain for the site of a capital or to choose that port instead of another (both Hokuriku and San-in, for example, have fine natural harbors, and their winters are no more severe than those on the opposite coast), to agree where to build the

roads as some new region is opened up—these were irrevo-
cable decisions that later events have generally approved.
Nevertheless, it is on the Pacific and the Inland Sea that
all the important elements of Japanese life have come to
be concentrated. The regions distant from those shores
now find themselves increasingly isolated.

✦ 11

Birth of the Megalopolis

THE DISPARITY between the relatively homogeneous group of key regions and the neglected regions, so widely dispersed and diverse in character, is now so pronounced that we need a simpler and more precise classification of zones than the conventional one we have been using— one that will clearly dissociate the vast urban and industrial belt stretching from Tokyo Bay to Ariake Bay in Kyushu from the rest of the country. For this we can borrow the term J. Gottman employed when he described the Boston–Washington zone in the United States: we can say a great "megalopolis" is being born on these Japanese shores.* It has already gathered into a few thousand square miles a large part of the country's population and economic power, a chain of cities, factories, and sprawling residential areas; it has erased almost every trace of rural life within its borders and has attracted a large labor force from every corner of the archipelago. This phenomenon is the major development in Japanese geography in the second half of the twentieth century.

*J. Gottmann, *op. cit.*

Inside this densely populated and industrialized belt are four centers that have existed since early times and that have managed to retain their preeminence and leadership. As we have seen, these are the Tokyo Bay area (Tokyo–Yokohama–Chiba), the urban region of Nagoya, the cluster of cities in Kansai (Kyoto–Osaka–Kobe), and the industrial agglomeration on the Straits of Shimonoseki (Shimonoseki–Kitakyushu–Fukuoka). They represent the heart and brains of the megalopolis and must be described before discussing the newer cities.

The "Ancient" Metropolises

THE TOKYO AGGLOMERATION

Although there was a castle on the site as early as

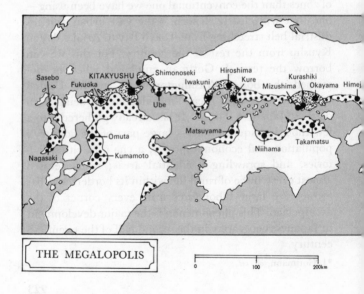

THE MEGALOPOLIS

0   100   200km

1457, the fortunes of Edo date from the establishment of the Tokugawa court in 1603. In 1600, three protective walls surrounded the city; the outermost was 15 miles in circumference. At the center was (and still is) the Imperial Palace. Edo remained the feudal capital until 1868. By the middle of the eighteenth century it already had 1 million inhabitants. After the 1868 Restoration, when it became the capital of a modern, centralized state, its progress was even more rapid, and today's Tokyo, with its population of 12 million, is perhaps the largest city in the world. It is the business center of the nation as well as its industrial, financial, and intellectual capital.

The city has known some tragic moments. The great earthquake of 1923 and the wartime bombardments of

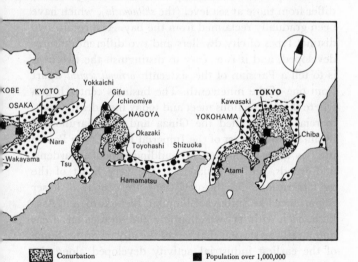

Conurbation

Population density over 700 per km²

Population over 1,000,000

Population over 150,000

1943–45 were the most devastating, but each time Tokyo recovered and again began to grow—without much thought to urban planning, however. In each of the ten years that followed the war, close to 100,000 homes were built; by 1955 the urban area, including the two neighboring prefectures, contained 15 million inhabitants. From 1955 to 1965 the city grew another one-quarter in size, and as the center became saturated the outskirts were invaded.

While the city is remarkably situated—Tokyo Bay is at the very center of the archipelago—the site itself is not particularly favorable. A marshy plain abuts on a shallow sea; the Musashino terrace, however, reaches all the way to the bay, where it is ruffled by some small hills on which part of the city stands. These slightly elevated quarters of the city (known as the *yamanote*) differ from those at sea level (the *shitamachi*), which have been gradually reclaimed from the bay. As a result, two distinct types of city dwellers and two different cultures developed, and it is as easy to distinguish the two as it is to tell a Parisian of the sixteenth *arrondissement* apart from one of the nineteenth. The business center began where the two sections meet and today includes the commercial artery called the Ginza and the Marunouchi business district, east of the Imperial Palace. The Palace itself is a vast complex of buildings, moats, gardens, and woods, and is situated at the very heart of the agglomeration. On the periphery are centers of lesser importance like Shibuya, Shinjuku, Ikebukuro, and Asakusa, each with its own shopping and amusement areas and a railway station that serves the city environs. Some of the earliest industrial activity developed along the bay to the south, in Kawasaki and Yokohama, but today it is moving northeast and settling on both shores of the Boso Peninsula in Chiba Prefecture.

The expansion of industry in the bay area has greatly increased traffic in the four ports of the agglomeration: Yokohama, Kawasaki, Tokyo, and Chiba. From a total of 165 million tons in 1964 it reached 450 million tons in 1975. The older industries of steel, iron, nonferrous metals, chemicals, and ceramics are found on extensive polders, the most recent of which, near Chiba, are also the site of new steel and petrochemical mills. An exception is the automobile industry, which was set up inland near Tachikawa. These industrial installations form a solid ring around the bay and cut off the city, the residential outskirts, and the countryside from any direct contact with the sea. Projects are being considered that call for filling in part of the bay and crossing it with bridges and express highways. Pending approval, the Tokyo Metropolitan Government is executing what is already a spectacular program of public works. It is building an extensive network of overhead express highways and an underground transportation system that will radiate from the Ginza–Nihonbashi district at the heart of the city; a second airport at Narita, about two hours from Tokyo, has just been completed. The Narita airport has double the capacity of the one on the bay at Haneda (halfway to Yokohama), which was constructed before World War II.

Yokohama was a mere fishing village when the treaties of 1859 opened it to foreigners, who proceeded at once to erect business houses on shore and to start to trade. As the deep-water port of Tokyo it grew rapidly: it had 450,000 people in 1927, and 850,000 in 1938. The population of 2.5 million attributed to it today is less significant, however, because the development of Kawasaki has made Yokohama an integral part of Tokyo. Yokohama's energetic port traffic has already been mentioned; its great volume, in turn, has attracted some of the major industries. The steel mills, the petrochemicals, and the Navy yards at Harima, Negishi, Uraga, and Yokosuka were established either close to the port or near Kawasaki, which has become the most active manufacturing area of the agglomeration.

Despite its short history, the agglomeration presents a far from uniform appearance. The "old" quarters of Yokohama and Tokyo, composed of traditional single-story houses sometimes set in tiny gardens, still exist alongside the ultramodern constructions that line the waterfront and between tall buildings of concrete and glass. By the early 1970s, skyscrapers, their tops lost in smoke and smog, had begun to rise in widely scattered sections of Tokyo, and their number is increasing each year. The immense conurbation today presents a scene of feverish activity.

THE KANSAI CONURBATION: KYOTO–OSAKA–KOBE

Like Tokyo and Yokohama, Osaka and Kobe form a single agglomeration, the great commercial center of which is similarly tied to its deep-water port. Here, however, urbanization began much sooner than in Kanto; it was close to these shores, possibly as early as the fourth century A.D., that the first capital of the country was founded. Osaka is situated on the delta of the Yodo River, which is the terminal point on the Inland Sea of the central Kansai corridor. On this marshy plain the city has built a canal network over which towers a great castle erected at the end of the sixteenth century by the warrior Hideyoshi. A wide boulevard runs north and south through the business quarter and connects the railroad station with the retail district of Shin-saibashi. This important artery continues north to the Shin-Osaka station of the New Tokaido Line and the commercial area surrounding it, while to the south it terminates at the port.

The port itself, often dredged, assumed importance only when the adjacent shores began to be systematically developed. The great industrial polders have kept encroaching upon the sea, and there are plans today to extend them even further. The traffic of the Osaka–Kobe agglomeration is about 250 million tons per year, to which must be added, of course, an enormous industrial output—the second largest in the country. Every type of manufacture is produced here; as in the capital, there is a clear distinction between the older industries such as textiles, which are found inland, and the more recent steel and petrochemicals, which were established on some 40 miles of seashore stretching from Sakai to beyond Kobe.

Such rapid growth has raised some serious problems. World War II bombing almost completely destroyed the city which, in 1945, was reduced to one million inhabitants. The center of Osaka was rebuilt on a more pretentious scale that linked it to the periphery: the streets were widened, overhead expressways were erected, and a subway was built. This periphery grew rapidly; large residential areas spread over the hills on the north, east, and south sides of the city as well as onto the plains leading to Nara on the one side and Kyoto on the other. The air over Osaka is as polluted as any in the country, and the gradual subsidence of the ground in the center of the city as a result of excessive drainage, from 1 to 1.75 inches per year in certain places, is among the more immediate problems.

Kobe is the best situated of all the cities of Japan; it lies on the lower slopes of Mt. Rokko, and the deep water immediately offshore makes it an exceptionally fine port. It was opened in Janurary 1868 to foreign commerce and was linked to Osaka by railway seven years later. It surpassed Yokohama in importance after the 1923 earthquake that destroyed three-quarters of that city. Kobe's maritime activity encouraged the development of much larger industries than Osaka's: 40 percent of them employ more than 1,000 workmen, as opposed to 23 percent in Osaka. These factories turn out petrochemicals, rubber, and heavy metal products used principally for shipbuilding. The city is also one of the main ports of entry, particulary for foodstuffs. Several parallel breakwaters protect the city from the open sea, while Mt. Rokko shelters it from the winds from the north and west. The port is being rapidly extended in the direction of Osaka, and one of the most important features is a large artificial island constructed of earth and rock which were transported directly by conveyer belt from nearby inland hills. Heavy industry now occupies the island and new docks provide miles of piers for berthing container ships.

Kobe forms a pattern of narrow bands that lie parallel to the shore—the port first, then the industrial zone, the commercial district at the foot of Mt. Rokko, and finally the residential area on the slope itself. Space here is limited, more so than in any other Japanese city. When the New Tokaido Line was extended west of Osaka, a tunnel almost eight miles long had to be built under Mt.

Rokko to avoid passing through the city. It was the least expensive alternative.

Kyoto, the third urban center of the Kansai region, presents a still different appearance. Laid out in A.D. 794 to duplicate the checkerboard design of Chang'an, the capital of the Sui Kingdom of China, the city lies on a long, narrow plain some 30 miles north of Osaka. It was the nation's imperial capital for more than ten centuries (794–1868) and has stayed aloof from the great industrial movements that have swept the country in modern times, despite its more than 1 million inhabitants. Like Peking, Rome, and Athens, it contains some of the world's greatest architectural treasures; it was spared the wartime air raids and therefore still retains the charm and beauty of an earlier age. To that past it also owes its skillful handicrafts, its pottery, basket weaving, paper, and especially its silk brocades. Nevertheless, some small pharmaceutical and electronic appliance factories have begun to appear in the southern part of the city. There are not enough of them to pollute the air, so the sky over the old city is generally clear. Tourism is still the chief commercial activity; there are a great many hotels, and each year some 10 million travelers pass through, principally in the spring (40 percent) and autumn. Southeast of the former Imperial Palace is a small modern quarter with new buildings, department stores, banks, and hotels; this area is surrounded by acres of old wooden houses, each with gray tile roofs. Since 1955, however, Kyoto has become part of the Osaka conurbation, functioning as a bedroom city, and its suburbs keep spreading in the two directions of Kobe and Lake Biwa. With Kobe and Osaka it constitutes the second great urban complex, covering some 30 miles from north to south and nearly 40 miles along the Inland Sea. To the east, beyond the heights that protect the Lake Biwa basin, lies the Nagoya region.

THE URBAN REGION OF NAGOYA

Nagoya is the central metropolis of a conurbation that covers the three prefectures of Gifu, Aichi, and Mie and that is populated by more than 3 million inhabitants. Unlike its two prestigious rivals, at the time of the Restoration it was merely the feudal capital of a province and no larger than Shizuoka or Kanazawa. The city, however was astride the Tokyo–Osaka axis and particpated in its prosperity. Here, more than in any other city, men of vision were able to follow, if not anticipate, the progress of the country and contribute important urban improvements of their own. Situated at the foot of Sekigahara Pass at a junction on the Tokaido for travelers en route to the Ise shrines and the Kii Peninsula, Nagoya developed rapidly and within a century grew from 120,000 inhabitants to 2 million for the agglomeration as a whole. Actually this was the result of the merger of two cities: the pilgrimage center of Atsuta and the feudal city a few miles away. When Atsuta was annexed in 1907, the city gained a waterfront and a port while the commercial center flourished on the terrace behind, in the shadow of the great castle to the north.

There is no finer business center in all Japan. It spreads over a grid of handsome avenues lined with department stores, hotels, banks, and wholesale firms, and is crowded with the heavy traffic that flows between the castle and the railway station. South of the railway line and extending to the sea is a totally different area, the industrial quarter, scored by canals and railroad tracks. For many years the railways supported the business of the city, which consisted mainly of transshipping. The lack of coal and the slow development of the port at first limited industry to light manufactures—to cotton in particular, for which the city still remains the biggest center in Japan. Since 1950, however, Nagoya has been spectacularly successful in both manufacturing and commerce.

Many square miles of Ise have been reclaimed and immense polders built that extend south to the cities of Yokkaichi and Tsu and southeast in the direction of Gamagori. The scene is similar to any reclaimed area of the postwar period: a complex of steel mills, shipyards, and petrochemical plants; the docks along the shore busy with the traffic of tankers, ore carriers, and container ships. This huge area includes an inner port with water over 30 feet deep and an outer port where the largest ships, drawing over 45 feet, can tie up to the docks. A 1968 forecast that the annual port traffic of 55 million tons of merchandise would double by 1975 was realized in 1973 when port traffic reached 130 million tons. The following figures reflect the progress of the local industry: metals alone rose from 11.6 percent in 1966 to 23 percent in 1970; machine tools rose from 22.7 to 34 percent in the same period. Metallurgy and chemicals together represent two-thirds of all industry in the Nagoya district. In the same period textiles declined from 17 to 6.5 percent and other light industries from 50 to 30 percent.

The Nagoya conurbation extends across the Nobi Plain to Gifu in the north and Ogaki in the west. It includes the old textile city of Toyohashi, the ceramics center at Seto, and the largest automobile assembly plants in the country at Toyota; to the south, new areas are constantly being occupied by heavy industry and petrochemicals manufacturing. Commuter trains, bus lines, and a subway system serve the urban zone. A number of public works have contributed to the district's expansion, one of the most important being an enormous breakwater which finally, in 1964, gave protection to the city from the typhoons that sweep in from Ise Bay. As in Tokyo and Osaka, satellite cities have been laid out on the adjacent hills to relieve the congestion in the older sections of the conurbation.

KITAKYUSHU–FUKUOKA

The fourth great urban and industrial center of Japan lies at the western end of the Inland Sea, on the Straits of Shimonoseki that separate Honshu from Kyushu. It embraces the big fishing port of Shimonoseki, the industrial agglomeration of Kitakyushu across the straits, the inland coal fields of Chikuho, and, somewhat further to the west, the large commercial and administrative center of Fukuoka. In all, there are some 3 million inhabitants. Kitakyushu, with a population of 1.4 million, was formed in 1963 by merging the five neighboring cities of Moji, Kokura, Tobata, Yahata, and Wakamatsu. It is connected with Shimonoseki by three undersea tunnels—two for the railways, the other for vehicles—and a suspension bridge which connects Tokyo and Osaka by express highway with the cities of Kyushu. Kitakyushu ranks seventh in Japan in the number of workers employed, sixth in the consumption of raw materials, and fifth in value added to its manufactures.

At the heart of the agglomeration are the Yahata steel mills, established by the Meiji government in 1901. Until 1926, Yahata produced 80 percent of the pig iron and 65 percent of the steel in Japan. (As late as 1960, it still supplied one-third of the pig iron, although by that time the mills of Tokyo and Osaka had surpassed it in steel production.) Before long, Yahata had added machine tools, heavy chemicals, and cement to its iron and steel output. The conditions were then favorable: coal from the Chikuho fields, while difficult to mine, was close by and abundant, as were the clay and limestone beds; ships carrying the necessary minerals and scrap iron could dock easily to unload; and the area lay in the path of Japanese manufactured products on their way to the ports of Asia. Since the end of World War II, however, these advantages have gradually disappeared. Whereas in 1938 the city produced 9 percent of all Japanese manufactures (value added), today the figure is 4.5 percent. The reasons for the decline, as indicated in Chapter 8, are many: the scarcity of fresh water; the distance from other industrial centers of the country; the shallowness and silting of the port; the lack of land on which to develop; and, more generally, the serious handicap that a manufacturing center suffers when, born in the age of coal, it tries to compete in a period that depends for most of its energy on petroleum.

The urban landscape here is unique in Japan and can be compared only to the Ruhr or the Midlands of Western Europe. Here are the same slag heaps, the same monstrous piles of ore and coal, the same sludgy canals, and the same forest of tall chimneys trailing dense plumes of smoke. The old feudal castle of Kokura is an island in this sea of disparate buildings. At the center of the agglomeration is the port of Dokai and on its shores stand the Yahata steel mills. Through this busy port enter the coking coal, the minerals, the scrap iron, and the lumber; from it are shipped the pig iron and steel for processing in the industrial centers of Osaka–Kobe, Nagoya, Tokyo, and the new manufacturing complex on the Inland Sea.

Not many miles away is Fukuoka, a "clean" city, born in the shadow of a feudal castle of the same name and situated close to the old port of Hakata. It is the commercial, banking, and intellectual center of Kyushu and the true capital of the region. A network of railways ties it to the other cities of the island. In addition to its service functions, Fukuoka also does some light manufacturing in factories of moderate size. The city is situated at the extreme western end of the Japanese megalopolis, but it is only two hours from Tokyo by plane and one from Osaka. In 1975 it was joined to these two cities by an extension of the New Tokaido Line; hence, by railroad it is only seven hours away from the capital, five from Nagoya, four from Osaka, and a little over one hour from Hiroshima.

The New Agglomerations

In the intervals between the four great metropolises, as well as in the region north of Tokyo, are a number of provincial capitals that approach the one-million mark in population. They form a further chain of urban centers within the megalopolis.

KYUSHU AND THE CHUGOKU DISTRICT

Southwest of Fukuoka, between Ariake Bay and the port of Sasebo, is the western anchor of the new chain. There are three agglomerations in the area, some 40 miles from each other: the industrial center of Omuta–Miike and the ports of Nagasaki and Sasebo. Omuta–Miike exists because of the presence of coal that in turn created a chemical industry. Recently the introduction of thermal power and the establishment of an aluminum industry have brought new life to these "black lands" that are dominated today by the Mitsui interests. The port of Nagasaki (500,000 population) at the head of a ria, together with the neighboring city of Isahaya (150,000), form a conurbation that soon will include the manufacturing district of Omuta and its maritime basin and extend up to the city limits of Sasebo (300,000), formerly an important naval base known for its shipyards. Unlike other future metropolises of 1 million or more, the Sasebo–Nagasaki–Omuta zone is still only loosely integrated. Bathed by the calm waters of Omura Bay and sheltered by the volcanic heights on Unzen Peninsula, it may someday become the southwestern anchor of the Japanese megalopolis.

Across the Straits of Shimonoseki from Kitakyushu are the industrial towns of the Ube coal basin, the petrochemicals center of Iwakuni, and, still further east, the city of Hiroshima. This old feudal capital, so tragically destroyed in 1945, was quickly rebuilt and by 1950 had become a modern city with a population of 250,000. Today the conurbation of Hiroshima has close to 1 million inhabitants and is constantly growing with the flood of immigrants from the mountains of Chugoku and San-in. It is unfortunately situated on a delta hemmed in by steep slopes. The Ota River flows down into a shallow bay that continually fills with silt. In order to grow the city has had to advance along the Inland Sea coast, in the direction of Miyajimaguchi to the west and the old port of Kure to the east, or to creep up the narrow serpentine valleys that lead inland. Hiroshima is an industrial, administrative, and educational center as well as an active port. It has neither raw materials nor sources of energy. Its chief activities, the manufacture of Toyo Kogyo automobiles within the city limits and the naval shipyards at Kure, are due mainly to its position astride the Japanese industrial axis. It is very modern in appearance, and only the old castle, rebuilt in concrete, is a reminder of the feudal past. To the south, the industrial zone and port area lie between the city and the sea where the famous oyster beds are still being cultivated, though these beds are threatened by the increasing pollution of the waters. Despite its many fine, wide avenues, the city has a serious traffic problem, which a subway system presently under consideration is expected to solve.

In the direction of Osaka, 125 miles to the east, another urban zone is rapidly taking shape on the shores of the Inland Sea. At the heart of it reposes the feudal city of Okayama (population 250,000). Okayama lies between an old alluvial plain and the rice paddies on Kojima Bay which were reclaimed from the sea in feudal times. On the eastern edge of the city stand the ancient castle and popular Korakuen Park on the banks of the Asahi River. Some 12 miles to the west is Kurashiki (population, 200,000). In feudal times Kurashiki was the port from which the rice of the region was shipped to Kansai; it has preserved an ancient quarter of old houses, once the homes of wealthy merchants, on the banks of the now-deserted canals. Here, some fifty years ago, an enterprising family named Ohara established a rayon factory that is today the largest in the nation.

The third unit of this conurbation is composed of the modern industrial zones of Konan and Mizushima. The former is merely the port of Okayama; Mizushima, on the other hand, represents the most spectacular industrial development of postwar Japan. It continues to grow at the expense of the sea, and the reclaimed lands are a complex of petroleum refineries and heavy chemical factories. Here also are large steel mills and many modest establishments producing plastics, diesel motors, and tractors. The water at the outer piers has been dredged to a depth of 52 feet to accommodate the largest freighters and their cargoes. Eventually the Okayama agglomeration as a whole will extend almost 25 miles along the shores of the Inland Sea, incorporating the ports of Tamano and Uno and the smaller center of Saidaiji. The New Tokaido Line now connects the city with Tokyo in just four hours.

Between Okayama and Kobe lies a fourth industrial and urban zone which also began as a feudal capital. Himeji can still boast about its medieval castle, the biggest in all Japan. The city has become an important commercial market and distribution center for the products of the mountain regions of east Chugoku and Tamba. The zone includes Harima, a district on the coast known for its steel and machine tools and which also manufactures textiles, chemical products, and foodstuffs. This industrial zone is a little over 20 miles from Akashi, the most westerly of Kobe's environs, and although the population is still only 500,000, it is a fully developed urban center lying between the two great conurbations of Okayama and Osaka.

THE TOKAI DISTRICT

Some 40 miles south of Nagoya lies the fourth of the future agglomerations of over 1 million inhabitants. It will absorb the present cities of Toyohashi and Hamamatsu, 20 miles apart and with populations of 250,000 and 450,000 respectively. Toyohashi was an important silk-reeling center in the days when the region of Ise Bay was reputed for its sericulture. Since the war it has diversified its activities and now produces cotton goods, foodstuffs, and wood products. It is separated from Hamamatsu by Lake Hamana (18,280 acres). This lake is ringed by a wide belt of pines, and the great natural beauty of the area has made it a popular tourist resort. The lake will be an important source of light and water at the heart of the agglomeration that one day will include Hamamatsu on its eastern border. This city was once a great cotton center but today has a wide range of manufactures. In fact textiles employ only one-quarter of the labor force, either in very large spinning mills or smaller weaving and dyeing establishments. Today the principal manufactures are electrical appliances, photographic and optical goods, cycles, and musical instruments. (The Yamaha and Kawai companies turn out an average of 250,000 pianos a year.)

About 45 miles further east on the coast in the direction of Tokyo is the feudal city of Shizuoka that will become the core of another agglomeration of over 1 million inhabitants. This one will contain Shizuoka itself (with its population of 300,000), the port of Shimizu and its heavy industries (5 miles away), the big fishing port of Yaezu, and the old manufacturing towns of Shimada and Fujieda. The tourist district of the Nihondaira will provide green space at the heart of the agglomeration, and the fine beaches of Omaezaki, still unfrequented, will someday be popular. This Shizuoka complex is the most westerly of the three industrial and urban zones that surround Suruga Bay. At the head of the bay, straddling the Fuji River and reaching to the foot of the famous mountain of the same name, lies the Gakunan district that includes the communities of Fuji, Yoshiwara, and Fujinomiya. The region was once known for its silk-spinning and weaving mills, but these have been replaced by a number of other industries, of which paper pulp and machine tools are the most important. Finally, less than 15 miles further east is the city of Numazu, which manufactures rubber, chemical products, and especially machine tools in factories of moderate size. These three industrial centers, very close to one another, together extend about 50 miles around Suruga Bay to form a solid band of industrial establishments some 80 miles from Tokyo.

NORTH OF TOKYO

North of Tokyo lies the relatively empty region of Tohoku. The megalopolis has been left behind; here is a natural coastline, extending for a great many miles and bare of any new construction. Urbanization is found only in certain widely scattered areas, but it needs little imagination to foresee the advance of the megalopolis into this district. While a manufacturing center has already appeared at Utsunomiya, in the northern corner of the Kanto Plain, the clearest indications are on the Pacific littoral, thus duplicating in the north the "inner-outer" juxtaposition we have seen elsewhere. There is first, 50 miles northeast of the capital, the important center of Kashima, reclaimed from the sea; the tall chimneys of its heavy metals and petrochemicals plants tower above the quiet delta of the Tone River. Further north are the heavy machinery plants at Hitachi, erected at the beginning of the century by private enterprise, that turn out the biggest generators and turbines in Japan.

Still further north the old Joban coalfields are dotted with factories now using thermal electricity.

Only Sendai, 225 miles north of Tokyo, appears to be a potential metropolis. It is already the intellectual center of the Tohoku region. Situated on a hill some 5 miles from the sea, it was once the seat of the most powerful daimyo of north Japan and had its beginning in the shadow of his castle. The city was destroyed during the Second World War, then rebuilt and laid out in a checkerboard of streets and broad avenues that feature a university and a large commercial district. By 1969 the population had passed the 500,000 mark. Sendai is gradually absorbing the neighboring communities and before long will be a well-integrated urban complex. The port of Shiogama has already been incorporated and the open country between is being staked out by industry. Most of the new development is taking place on the Pacific coast around famous Matsushima Bay, a popular tourist resort known also for its oyster and seaweed beds, and to the north as far as the fishing port of Ishinomaki. The latter, according to present plans, will one day become an important center of industry and fishing. It lies 12 miles from Shiogama, a mere 20 miles from the center of Sendai, and will form the northern anchor of an agglomeration whose very existence will depend heavily upon the sea.

Still further north the coast is rugged and sparsely inhabited except for the old steel town of Kamaishi and the fishing port of Hachinohe, which has become a busy industrial center due in large part to its new petrochemicals industry. But one has to cross the Tsugaru Straits to Hokkaido to find the sort of dynamic urbanism that exists within the megalopolis. A whole chain of cities—

Hakodate, Otaru, Muroran, Tomakomai—all close to each other and with populations of 150,000 to 250,000 each, together form a solid industrial complex, with Sapporo clearly at the head. This city that in 1869 was a mere cluster of huts at a crossroads on a marshy plain is today an agglomeration of over 1 million inhabitants; it sprawls at the foot of some low hills on the edge of the great Ishikari Plain, 20 miles inland from its own port of Otaru. The streets and wide avenues were laid out in straight lines to resemble the prairie cities of North America; the buildings are modern and the homes, erected to withstand the rigors of winter, differ radically in structure from the traditional Japanese house. A subway line was inaugurated in December 1971, and an ambitious urban project has begun to supply heat to the commercial district and eventually to the residential areas.

The Japan Sea is ten miles northwest of Sapporo. The Pacific is south of the city at the end of a long plain on which stands Chitose and Sapporo's airport. On this south coast is Tomakomai, Japan's great paper and pulp center. The city has bold plans for creating a heavy industry, the plants to be erected around a large artificial port gouged out of the coastal plain. Thirty miles to the southwest at the old coaling port and steel city of Muroran (population 250,000), the seashore is being reclaimed and the polders made ready for a new industrial center.

Recent Changes: The Genesis of the Megalopolis

The gradual transformation of the country along the Tokyo–Nagasaki axis and, in a less orderly fashion, around Sendai and Sapporo, has profound significance.

Whether it be the birth of a metropolis or the development of a bay, everywhere the same changes are taking place. At first the purpose was to increase land area at the expense of the sea, the mountain, or the paddy. Rice fields were filled in and raised about three feet to support small, conventional houses or a new housing development; blocks of buildings three or four stories high were aligned on the sea front or the slope of a hill. Where space was limited—as on the shore at Miyajimaguchi near Hiroshima, for example—the hills were simply leveled.

It is on the coast, however, that the transformation is most striking. Long concrete dikes have been built either along the shore, enclosing bays and coves, or parallel to the beach and several hundred yards offshore, where they form large artificial islands slashed by wide channels that provide new industrial sites and docking facilities. Tokyo Bay; the bays of Suruga, Nagoya, and Osaka; the shores of Himeji, Mizushima, Hiroshima, and Iwakuni—each presents the same profile of tall furnaces and cracking towers.

The railroad and highway that used to run along the shore must now pass inland, between the busy industrial belt and the open country where rice is still planted and harvested each year. Here a new world has been born between the mountain and the sea, a world half rural, half urban, in which the farmer setting out for his fields each day crosses the path of the workman on his way to the factory.

ECONOMIC ASPECTS

As we have said, this transformation of the land was mainly the work of large Japanese companies which chose those areas they considered most suitable for the location of their huge installations. That they were encroaching upon rural land could not be helped. They had to find room at all costs, for the economic future of the country depended on it. The projects were of so vast a scale that they could be undertaken only by the very biggest companies, by combines corresponding to former zaibatsu like the Mitsui, Mitsubishi, Sumitomo empires, or by some huge new arrival like the Idemitsu Petroleum Company.

The composition of the Mizushima complex is a good example. Here, working side by side, are petroleum and chemical product manufacturers like Mitsubishi Sekiyu, Mitsubishi Kasei, Nihon Gosei Kagaku, Nihon Polymer, and Nihon Carbide. Across the Inland Sea, in Shikoku's Niihama complex, the pattern is repeated: Sumitomo Kagaku (heavy chemicals), Sumitomo Kozan (copper ore), and Sumitomo Kyodo Denryoku (electricity) are all participants. This list of companies illustrates the practice, quite common among the subsidiaries of a former zaibatsu, of joining forces on a given project for the sole purpose of financing it and sharing the profits. In the case of Niihama, all the companies stem from the parent Sumitomo group and bear its name; yet even here, while sharing the heavy costs, they remain legally and administratively independent.

Groups such as these, concerned with heavy industry, are called *combinato* (combines) by the Japanese. The term does not imply interdependence; the companies have come together simply to pool the capital necessary to initiate and carry out a project. These projects can be extremely costly. First a site must be selected with manufacturing and distributing facilities in mind—a waterfront site (since most of the product will be moved by sea) with easy access to the hinterland and plenty of fresh water and power. Then the enormous engineering task must be financed, expensive distillation plants built on the seashore if fresh water is scarce, and the channels deepened to permit the approach of tankers and ore barges, particularly in the Inland Sea where large ships cannot navigate without first dredging the area.

Before a new industrial zone is created in an appropriate location, there must be very careful planning. The decisions are reached by consensus, and the choice of a site such as Mizushima or Kashima, for instance, is made only after years of study. The industries that are established generally require a great deal of land and, like steel or petrochemicals, are of the kind that business leaders consider essential to the country's industrial life. In few nations of the nonsocialist world have the country's economic needs led to the systematic survey and development of such vast areas of the homeland.

The interior of the country, on the other hand, has been little affected by the close presence of these combines, at least insofar as daily life and productivity are concerned. The fruit orchards and market gardens on the slopes of Tokai and San-yo flourished before their arrival and continue to produce for a ready market. Across the highway that separates the farmer from the new factories, rice is cultivated as it has been from time immemorial. Moreover, thanks to a rise in the price of the farmer's produce and the value of his land, he is now prosperous and sees no advantage in becoming a laborer.

DEMOGRAPHIC AND RESIDENTIAL ASPECTS

The Japanese megalopolis contains almost half the

population of the country. Its industry attracts large numbers from other regions of the archipelago. From early times, the inhabitants of the interior and of the "inner" zone have migrated to the metropolises on the shores of the Pacific and Osaka Bay. Since 1955, however, instead of looking to the big cities many people are now settling in intermediate areas that are only slightly urbanized and where the average income is consequently lower. More significant to them than income is the low level of industrialization; this seems to be a determining factor in much recent migration. Numbers of young workmen are also leaving metropolises like Osaka or Kawasaki—where the air even on the outskirts is polluted and unhealthy—for "young" regions that are peaceful and bright and where pleasant living conditions will compensate them for the difference in income. A dual trend is apparent in these present-day population movements; in addition to the traditional "descent" from the mountains to the coastal cities, there is now this lateral displacement from one city to another or from a city to some rural area that is becoming urbanized.

In these new youthful communities, changes in the administrative structure follow, belatedly as usual. Old villages become towns, then cities, before they have had time to develop a proper core or center. What becomes the social center, therefore, is no longer the village, the neighborhood, or the apartment house these young people had previously known; it is the *kaisha*, the company that recruited them and that now employs and houses them. The new arrivals quickly adopt the social pattern that a Japanese fits into wherever he is: the personal and hierarchical relationships within the group where each one's place is recognized and fixed by custom.

Because of the growing population new homes have
had to be built in the megalopolis, either in the intervals
between cities or in the hearts of the cities themselves.
Architects are given free rein, and the result is an interesting preview of the engineering techniques and building methods of the Japan of the future. Until about 1960,
the traditional wooden house constituted 75 percent of all
new construction: today the figure is one-half. Steel and
concrete, which were popular long before World War II,
are now employed throughout the megalopolis in addition to wood. They are the materials commonly used in
the construction of the standard apartment house—100
to 130 feet long, with four floors and no elevator. Inside,
the apartments are generally designed to resemble the
traditional home. The bedroom floor is covered by
tatami, and sliding wood-and-paper partitions between
the rooms contribute to the versatility of the apartment.

In metropolises, glass and steel buildings of 10 and 15
or more floors are common, and they are fast replacing
the first generation of stone or concrete buildings popular
from 1935–45. These new angular city districts, quite
stark yet often quite handsome, at times straddle huge
underground shopping centers. Usually located directly
under or near one of the main railroad stations, such
centers in Osaka, Nagoya, Tokyo, and Sapporo provide
long, heated and air-conditioned galleries where pedes-
trians can shop and eat, circulate freely, and gain access
to subways or the buildings or stations above. The galleries at Sapporo and Osaka have circular ramps and
elaborate fountains, and, like the others, are subter-
ranean cities in themselves. The development of underground urbanism is a further example of the intensive use
of space that is characteristic of the megalopolis.

From the busy city centers the subways continue to extend their services in order to keep up with the retreating outskirts. These in turn often have to be remodeled, for some of them are quite old, even unhealthy—their streets still lined with dilapidated buildings and unsightly factories. On the hills, at varying distances from the metropolis, residential communities are springing up, generally around railroad stations. At the same time a growing number of summer homes are appearing on the shores nearby (on the Miura, Ise, and Kii peninsulas) and turning once rural and forested land into extensions of urban prosperity. The Japanese seem not to mind living an hour or more away from the city, and their homes—often set in an attractive garden, as in Kamakura or Oiso—could easily be mistaken for summer cottages. High rents and building costs often oblige people to live far from their places of work. The municipalities of Tokyo, Nagoya, and Osaka have foreseen the need for satellite cities; well beyond their outskirts they have begun to build communities of 50,000 to 150,000, each with its own educational, commercial, and transportation facilities linking it to the metropolis. Examples of these satellite cities are Tama near Tokyo, Senri near Osaka, and Kozoji near Nagoya.

ASPECTS OF THE INTERRELATED LIFE

Scattered the length of the megalopolis, these great urban centers, industrial complexes, residential communities, and old and small cities all lie within a single narrow belt. This belt is never more than 6 or 7 miles wide except in the neighborhood of the metropolises. Generally less than 2 miles wide, it even disappears completely at times, as at Hakone Pass and Sekigahara or again on the coast between Himeji, Okayama, and Hiroshima. This makes for easy but not necessarily rapid communication. All the industrial establishments, the great combines in particular, depend upon the three command posts of Tokyo, Osaka, and Nagoya. Of the 100 leading Japanese companies capitalized at 1 billion yen (about $3.5 million) or more, 56 have their headquarters in Tokyo, 20 in Osaka, 7 in Nagoya, 2 each in Chugoku and Kyushu, 1 each in Hokkaido, Hokuriku, and Shikoku, and none in Tohoku. Sixty-three percent of the company directors live in Tokyo, 22 percent in Osaka, 4 percent in Nagoya, 2 percent in Kyushu, and 1 percent each in Hokkaido, Tohoku, Chugoku, and Shikoku. Half of the nation's bank loans are made to residents of Kanto—that is, Tokyo; one-quarter to those in Kansai, in Osaka and Kobe. In the offices of Tokyo's Marunouchi district and Osaka's Midosuji, and less often in Nagoya, the important decisions are made concerning the business activities of enterprises scattered the 625-mile length of the megalopolis. Since a company with business headquarters in Tokyo, Nagoya, or Osaka may have factories or offices in more than one place, a constant stream of planes and trains carries businessmen from one point to another within this three-city belt. Airlines handle part of this traffic, but most of it is carried by the New Tokaido Line express trains. Round trips are possible within the same day from Tokyo to Hiroshima and Fukuoka, and Sapporo will be equally accessible about 1980. There is also an express highway from the capital to Kobe that parallels this railway line and that is being extended along the shores of the Inland Sea.

Tokyo and Osaka retain their uncontested leadership at the heart of this huge complex. Osaka reigns over the western half of the country, and the capital dominates the northern half; Nagoya has reserved a place for itself in the intermediate zone. This gives urban Japan a hydra-headed structure that is not unique in the world (Brazil, Australia, the USSR, and China furnish other examples) but is of considerable importance nevertheless. If we equate Paris or London with Tokyo, and regional cities of over one million like Lyons, Marseilles, the Lille complex, Birmingham, Manchester, or Glasgow with Fukuoka, Hiroshima, or Sapporo, it is clear that Osaka and Nagoya represent two intermediate stages that are missing in the French and British urban hierarchy. Today the intricate web of people, capital, and enterprise that constitutes the megalopolis is rapidly becoming tighter and more resistant and is intensifying the division of the country into two very unequal parts: the immense rural regions that are the source of labor and the narrow urban and industrial strip that borders the Pacific and the Inland Sea.

+ 12

Future Trends and Developments

SO SWIFTLY does Japan change that a geographical study of the archipelago is like a snapshot blurred from rapid motion; it is impossible to reach any definite conclusions. Since the end of the Second World War, forces of immense power and unpredictable significance have been reshaping the crowded plains, the remote mountains, the barren solitudes of the north and the seas that bathe these shores. The future of physical Japan is closely tied to the country's economy, which never ceases to make spectacular changes in the topography. The impression we are given today is that of a power remarkably organized and self-controlled, a power that has succeeded in gathering the collective body into a community of common ideals, values, and objectives. Today's prosperity, however, is not without its dark clouds. The political problems of relations with the USSR, China, and the United States; the problem of primary and secondary industry, of the farmhands and small factory workers who will one day have to be integrated into society; the danger of an "overheated" economy; the impact since 1971 of international monetary problems;

252

the oil crisis and the recession that followed it; the grave deterioration of the natural environment—all of these pose more problems to Japan than its present progress appears to have solved.

More than ever, the country is subject to influences over which it has little control. In addition to domestic turmoils, the vagaries of international economics and politics are constantly threatening the basic conditions upon which Japan's growth depends. Japan's international relations grow in importance when we consider the relatively narrow range of conditions under which its economy can maintain itself.

Occasionally, however, extraneous circumstances have saved Japan from an impending crisis. In 1950, it was the Korean War; in 1956, the Suez crisis stimulated shipbuilding and the related steel industry; more recently, American purchases for the Vietnam war helped to check a recession that had started in 1962.

More often, though, the government must step in. The state not only develops economic overviews or long-term plans similar to the ones that rebuilt war-ravaged industries and then doubled the national income from 1960 to 1970, but it also responds to more immediate problems, as it did to the recent rise in the rate of inflation.

The rise in the inflation rate was not due solely to the cost increases imposed by the Arab oil exporters at the end of 1973. In fact, by the autumn of 1973, the Japanese import bill was already showing a disturbing rise due to the increasing cost of lumber, wheat, and metallic ore. Japanese wholesale prices at that time were 18 percent above the level of a year before. This was in sharp contrast to the preceding fifteen years of relative economic stability.

Following the oil-exporting nations' price hike, Japan had to pay $12 billion in 1974 just to maintain its imports at the 1973 level, forcing its one-time trade surplus into a deficit of $10 billion. The trade unions contributed to the galloping inflation by achieving a 32 percent wage boost in their 1974 "spring offensive."

The government responded to these two successive tremors, the sudden inflation of 1972 and the oil price hike of 1973, with a sharp turn toward austerity and emergency measures that included the imposition of price controls on large manufacturers. As a result, by the end of 1974 inflation was slackening, and the increase in exports had pushed the balance of payments into the black from its deficit of $10 billion.

Related problems remain, however. The unemployment rate, though moderated by the Japanese tradition of lifelong employment, was still at the 2 percent level in 1976. Wholesale prices continued to rise by less than 9 percent a year, but retail prices were still a big problem, despite the unions' settlement for wage hikes averaging less than 10 percent.

All in all, though, Japan seems to have coped with recession more successfully than other industrial countries. Showing confidence in the future (and under pressure from other governments), Japan's Finance Ministry has begun to liberalize its once severe restrictions on foreign capital investment in Japanese industries. In 17 categories, the capital invested can now be entirely foreign; in 33, it may be shared equally; in the rest, it can be 20 percent without need for prior government approval.

Frightened by the scale of American investments in Western Europe and fearful that some powerful overseas group will seize control of Japanese companies, Japanese industry has tended to react by merging, thus reviving the former zaibatsu. Outstanding examples are Nippon Steel, formed by combining Yahata and Fuji steel companies, and Mitsui Toatsu Chemicals, born of the recent merger of the Mitsui Chemical Industries and the Toyo Koatsu Industries. The latter combine will build ethylene factories capable of producing 300,000 tons per year, a figure which neither company could have accomplished alone and which will match the production of American competitors. On the other hand, the automobile makers are aware that their numbers are a threat to the industry. There are 11 car manufacturers for Japan's 100 million inhabitants; the United States, with more than double this population, has only 4.

To meet the foreign competition they anticipate, local plants are being automated and equipped with the most modern machinery. Another reason for automation, however, is strictly demographic. There is a growing concern about the rise in the average age of the nation's population. If present birth and death rates continue, the population will cease to increase after 1990; in that year it will be about 130 million. The average age will rise thereafter, and population will stabilize and then slowly decrease. By then the number of gainfully employed will be the same as at present: 59 million, ranging from 15 to 59 years of age; but the over-60 age group will have increased from 10 to 25 percent of the total population, and the under-15 will have declined from 35 to 18 percent. Taking the 1950 population figures as 100, by 2015 the under-15s will be 56 and the over-60s, 395.

Even if the labor situation were not ominous, from about 1965 until the oil crisis of 1973, fear of foreign competition in productivity would suffice to explain the present interest in automation. Some of the results have been remarkable. The Honda factory at Suzuka, near Nagoya, turns out a motorcycle every 10 seconds; 1,100 machine tools are used in the process (one-quarter made by Honda), enabling the company to insure such a production with a labor force of only 2,800, 61 percent of whom left school at the age of 18. In the three other Honda factories that manufacture motors, motor cars, and precision tools, similar stress is laid on productivity.

The Future for Trade

Foreign trade, which is vital to the country, can expect to see two immense and almost unexplored markets—the USSR and China—opened up as soon as the political climate is favorable. Negotiations with the USSR regarding the development of western Siberia (the petroleum fields of Tyumen), central Siberia (lumber and minerals), and eastern Siberia in particular (the natural gas in Sakhalin) have made little progress despite the great interest both parties manifest in the projects. For the present at least, Japan appears to have more to sell than to buy from the USSR and complains about the long-term credits the Soviets are demanding. The two nations have not yet signed a World War II peace treaty, nor have they solved the problem of fishing rights that arises between them year after year.

With China, the situation before 1972 was even more disappointing. Although Japan is Peking's principal trading partner and more than 2,800 Japanese firms were represented at the Canton Fair in 1975 (out of 30,000 foreign traders), the amount of business concluded yearly is small. The Chinese have always looked upon foreign trade as a sort of safety valve, never as a source of wealth, much less a necessary factor in the development of their country. Moreover, the concept of a consumer society is the antithesis of the Chinese ideal. Japanese political policy (its ties with the United States aside) arouses little confidence in Peking, which sees in Japan's struggle for economic power a revival of nationalism and a belated and frightening echo of the militarism of the 1930s.

There are, of course, many markets open to Japanese enterprise, and none is being overlooked on any of the continents. In Dusseldorf, New York, New Delhi, or São Paulo, the Japanese businessman is established in numbers, prospecting, collecting information and statistics, and displaying untiring diligence and skill. A little-known aspect of this expansion is his interest in the rural development of these countries. Mitsui Bussan in Sumatra and Mitsui Shoji and Ishikawajima–Harima in South Vietnam have built factories for the manufacture of agricultural tools and fertilizers and have started experimental farms. Other companies are growing rice or cotton in Iran or have ranches in Brazil and Paraguay; still others are watching the agricultural development of the Sudan. A group of 25 companies has completed plans for the agricultural development of Vietnam, to be carried out as soon as that nation normalizes its relations with Japan. These rural operations are on a large scale—250,000 acres planted in sorghum near Djakarta, 750,000 acres in cotton in Iran—and have led to the sale of many nonagricultural items; fertilizers arouse interest in a variety of chemical products, and tractors promote the sale of machine tools.

These important programs of technical and financial

aid and of agricultural and industrial investment, in both developed and underdeveloped countries, have encountered two major obstacles. The first is strictly economic. Japan faces intense competition from the great powers who are also sending capital, plants, and technicians to Asia, Africa, and Latin America. With each new contract the competition grows keener; the Japanese bids no longer win as easily as they did before the war, or even until 1960, because of the rising cost of raw materials and the higher wages at home. The second obstacle, still troublesome despite the passage of time, is psychological. Aggressive Japanese business methods, following so soon after a military presence that has not been entirely forgotten, shock those who still harbor some suspicions. The nations of Southeast Asia in particular are still far from ready to open wide their doors to Japanese enterprise.

The Domestic Scene

Over 80 percent of domestic production, however, is consumed by the Japanese themselves, and this domestic market is the manufacturer's main outlet. Rising wages have increased the demand for consumer goods of all types, and the rural population, supported by the government, enjoys a continually improving standard of living. The farmer is able to buy electrical appliances, automobiles, and better clothes—articles that until 1955 had been intended for the urban classes. In 1970 a saturation point seemed to have been reached, especially in the field of electronics (1.4 million color television sets in stock in February 1971) and electrical household appliances; domestic sales of automobiles rose only 4 percent from

1970 to 1971. But the consumption rise went on even during the black years beginning in 1972, and, in a repetition of the pattern seen in Europe and North America, Japanese are spending more on travel, recreation, and other services.

Many Japanese see this as proof of the enduring value of such traditions as the guarantee of lifelong employment and the art of accommodation between labor and management and among the big firms themselves. More than ever, the Japanese are eager to protect the spirit of cooperation that exists among all levels of society and to maintain the traditional social structure of the family, the business enterprise, and the local community. They are not eager to transform themselves into a totally Western democratic society, for it is precisely their distinctive past which gives them such confidence in the future.

What will the Japanese economy be like in 1980? Government economic planners, with the help of computers, project that the gross national product will increase at an annual average rate of 6 percent until 1980. Discounting inflation, this means that the GNP will rise 13 percent each year. Retail price increases will drop to the 6 percent level from the 10 percent level of 1976. Wholesale prices will in that same period drop to 4 percent. The rate of unemployment will fall to 1.3 percent in 1980, and the labor force will grow from 52.7 million to 55.6 million. The Government expects sufficient tax revenue to manage its deficit, for the tax burden of individuals and corporations will increase, as will social security contributions. The average 6 percent "real growth" of GNP means a per capita income of $6,600 in 1980, double the figure for 1975.

To attain this six-percent growth rate, half that of the

1960s, the Japanese economy will have to tread a relatively narrow path and the government will have to exercise cautious economic planning. This means that Japan has entered a new period of development and that there will have to be many readjustments. Some of the problems facing Japan depend directly or indirectly upon the international situation; others are the result of the nation's own rapid progress. Its difficulties today are in many ways the price it is paying for prosperity. From a geography point of view and in light of the facts and perspectives we have presented, these difficulties fall into two categories: problems of the environment, and problems in the development of the country—both arising out of the growth of the megalopolis.

THE ENVIRONMENT

In Japan, the problem of pollution looms larger than in any other nation because both the causes of pollution and half the country's population are found within the megalopolis. Pollution of the air and the waters, noises and odors, industrial wastes, and land subsidence in the cities are but some of the items on the list of catastrophes. Since 1960 the number of pollution victims has increased every year; unique maladies due to mercury or cadmium poisoning have already caused scores of deaths. Cases of asthma, bronchitis, pulmonary complaints, and eye and skin irritations are no longer even reported in industrial areas like Kawasaki or Osaka.

Japan's pollution, like that in most other places, comes in many varieties. Coal and steel areas such as Yahata in Kyushu and Muroran in Hokkaido have been plagued by the same sooty air that characterized the Midlands, the Ruhr, or Pittsburgh before 1960; with the replacement of coal by fuel oil these areas have of course improved.

City dwellers have their own unique mixture of noise, odors, automobile exhaust, and photochemical smog. In addition, they, too, are the victims of poisoned waters; the fish that are a major part of their diet often contain harmful amounts of mercury and other chemicals.

The fatal or crippling diseases that have appeared in Japan are directly traceable to large factories (often manufacturers of petrochemicals) that have dumped mercury and other wastes directly into streams or bays. People living in the area are poisoned directly by the water or indirectly by eating rice irrigated with the water or fish caught in the water. The prime offenders in this type of environmental destruction are the industrial "combines" that are springing up all along the urban corridor. Wherever they can, people are moving out of these areas because of noise, odors, and poison. But for every family that moves, there are many others that cannot.

The government has taken some action. The six most seriously affected areas have been given special protection. Since 1960 14 laws have been passed covering various aspects of the problem: control of smoke; payment by the responsible parties for damage caused by pollution; stricter regulations regarding water and food, disposal of industrial wastes, protection of cultivated lands from irrigation by polluted streams; and supervision of coastal waters. Public opinion has also awakened to the danger. Since 1970 several sensational cases have been tried in court and won by the plaintiffs who were able to prove that their or their relations' ailments were the result of industrial pollution; they received substantial compensation from the companies responsible. A very great deal remains to be done, however. There are almost as many varieties of pollution as there are manufacturing plants, and the megalopolis is experiencing a disproportionate amount of grave illness. The danger, unquestionably, is very real.

Japanese city dwellers have other problems as well, many of them the result of the cities' extremely dense populations. Streets are narrow and choked with cars, superhighways are few, and trains and subways, though plentiful, are always overcrowded. The housing shortage is serious, despite constant government efforts to solve it. Residential land prices have risen at such a steep rate that the number of property owners fell from 56 percent of the population in 1960 to 40 percent in 1970. More and more people are crowding into apartments that are further and further from their workplaces, and are paying higher and higher rents for them.

THE GROWTH OF THE MEGALOPOLIS

The second major problem raised by the megalopolis is of another order. We have already described the contrast—a contrast that becomes more pronounced every day—between this dense, narrow ribbon of cities and factories and the rest of the country. It can be the cause of grave difficulties, such as encouraging population movements from one part of the country to the other; creating underdeveloped zones like San-in, Tosan, south Kyushu, and central and western Tohoku; and causing an accumulation of all the nuisances mentioned above in the most thickly populated sectors of the country. To have a better understanding of the problems, the government in 1965 ordered the Planning Board to present a report on the "State of the Nation in 1985." Drawn from all the sources available to forecasters, the study predicts that by 1985 nine Japanese out of ten will be living in cities, with Tokyo and Osaka alone sheltering 25 million and 15 million respectively; that central Japan will be turning into a vast desert; and that three-quarters of the total population will be crowded, probably under dangerously unhealthy conditions, on the shores of the "outer" zone that extends from Tokyo (or Sendai) to Nagasaki.

To meet this threat, the government has selected a number of sites on which to establish infrastructures that will provide work for the local population; at the same time it wants to strictly control investments in the 4 zones it considers excessively urbanized: Tokyo–Yokohama, Nagoya, Osaka–Kobe, and Kitakyushu. The areas chosen total 18: 6 "priority zones of development" and 12 "urban industrial zones." The industrial zones lie outside the megalopolis and are scattered throughout the neglected regions: central Hokkaido; Hachinohe, Sendai Bay, and the Joban coalfields in Tohoku; Niigata and Toyama–Takaoka in Hokuriku; Lake Suwa and Matsumoto in Tosan; Ehime in Shikoku; Oita, Nobeoka–Hyuga, and Omuta in Kyushu. The 6 priority zones of development, on the other hand, lie between the major cities and threaten to stimulate the growth of the megalopolis. We have already encountered them: Kashima, Suruga Bay, and Mikawa Bay in the Nagoya region; Harima near Himeji; the Hiroshima region; and the Shunnan area which includes the coalfields of Ube. Another, more comprehensive plan has been proposed that would divide the country into 7 great zones to replace the regional divisions of today. Hokkaido would have

2 regions, one of them rural, the other urban and industrial. Tohoku would remain rural, although modernized.

It is not at all clear, however, whether these measures
will have much effect on the seemingly irreversible trend
toward settling and investing in the megalopolis. The
mixed results of such plans can already be seen in the vast
project for covering the archipelago with a network of
express highways and express trains of the New Tokaido
type, to connect all four islands and improve communications with Shikoku and Hokkaido in particular. This
plan is being pursued with the speed and skill the Japanese have already demonstrated. The lines most urgently
needed were built first, of course, and these are the ones
that now extend the length of the megalopolis. This has
encouraged further settlement within the belt and attracted more industry, setting at naught any influence
the other lines might have upon the development of the
neglected regions.

Thus these plans do not take the overall problem of
regional equilibrium into account. Fifty-four percent of
industrial production came from Tokyo, Osaka, and
Nagoya in 1955; twenty years later, it was 67 percent.
Local resistance, heightened by the great "pollution
trials" and the accelerating depopulation of the neglected
regions, led, in the midst of the production boom,
to another national plan in 1969 that aimed at spatially
"contracting" the archipelago by means of rapid transit
systems like the Shinkansen. In June of 1972, the then
Prime Minister Kakuei Tanaka produced his own plan
for remodeling the archipelago. His intention to move
industry into the rural areas accelerated the land specu-
lation that had begun in 1965 when businessman first
began to search for new investments in the countryside.

Prime Minister Tanaka's plan, like all the others, assumed that the booming economy would continue uninterrupted. The oil crisis and the following recession, however, made these plans obsolete almost overnight. In 1976, new projects with more moderate objectives were due to be drafted along guidelines proposed by official economists. But the weight of the past is so heavy that, for some time yet, the complete reorganization of the archipelago will likely only favor the megalopolis and allow it to pursue its progress. The Japan of the 1980s will probably be nothing more than a magnification of the Japan of today, for the formidable forces that draw people and their property to this clearly defined axis can no longer be denied. Crowded into their enormous cities, living under skies gray with smoke, breathing foul air, exposing their senses to the constant din, packed twice a day into their overtaxed commuter trains, the greater number of Japanese appear today to be the helpless victims of their own prosperity.

But Japan's prosperity is the fruit of a struggle against overpopulation and poverty that has lasted for centuries. Little more than one hundred years ago, when Japan's population was 30 million, newborn infants in the countryside were drowned because they could not be fed. Today 100 million live on the archipelago and enjoy a standard of living that is rising from day to day. In few places in the world, and certainly nowhere else in Asia, has man shown such ingenuity in transforming an ungrateful environment and making it possible for so many to live on so few acres under such unfavorable conditions. The Japanese have set an example for all nations to consider.

✦ Selected Bibliography

Beasley, W. G. *The Modern History of Japan*. New York: Praeger, 1963.

Benedict, Ruth. *The Chrysanthemum and the Sword*. Boston: Houghton Mifflin, 1946.

Borton, Hugh. *Japan's Modern Century*. New York: Ronald Press, 1955.

Dore, Ronald P. *Aspects of Social Change in Modern Japan*. Princeton: Princeton University Press, 1967.

Dore, Ronald P. *City Life in Japan*. London: Routledge and Kegan Paul, 1958.

Dore, Ronald P. *Land Reform in Japan*. London and New York: Oxford University Press, 1959.

Fairbank, John K.; Reischauer, Edwin O.; and Craig, Albert M. *East Asia: The Modern Transformation*. Boston: Houghton Mifflin, 1965.

Gottmann, J. *Megalopolis*. New York: Twentieth Century Fund, 1961.

Hall, John W., and Ward, Robert E. *Village Japan*. Chicago: University of Chicago Press, 1959.

Huddle, Norie; Reich, Michael; and Stiskin, Nahum. *Island of Dreams: Environmental Crisis in Japan*. New York and Tokyo: Autumn Press, 1975.

Japan Central Meteorological Office. *Climatographic Atlas of Japan*. Tokyo: Japan Central Meteorological Office, 1948.

267

Japan Economic Research Center. *Economic Planning and Macroeconomic Policy*. Tokyo: Japan Economic Research Center, 1971.

Japan Economic Research Center. *Japan's Economy in 1980 in the Global Context*. Tokyo: Japan Economic Research Center, 1972.

Kahn, Herman. *The Emerging Japanese Superstate: Challenge and Response*. Englewood Cliffs, N. J.: Prentice-Hall, 1970.

Kolb, Albert. *East Asia: Geography of a Cultural Region*. London: Methuen, 1971.

Lebra, Takie S., and Lebra, William P., eds. *Japanese Culture and Behavior: Selected Readings*. Honolulu: University Press of Hawaii, 1974.

Nakamura, Hajime. *The Ways of Thinking of Eastern Peoples*. Tokyo: Unesco, 1960.

Nakane, Chie. *Japanese Society*. London: Weidenfeld and Nicolson, 1970.

Noh, Toshio, and Gordon, Douglas H., eds. *Modern Japan: Land and Man*. Tokyo: Teikoku Shoin, 1974.

Reischauer, Edwin O. *Japan: Past and Present*. New York: Knopf, 1964.

Sansom, George B. *Japan: A Short Cultural History*, rev. ed. New York: Appleton-Century-Crofts, 1962.

Sansom, George B. *The Western World and Japan*. New York: Knopf, 1951.

Taeuber, Irene. *The Population of Japan*. Princeton: Princeton University Press, 1958.

Tanaka, Makoto. *Nihon Kokusei Zue*. Tokyo: Kokuseisha, 1976 (in Japanese).

Teikoku Shoin (staff). *Atlas of Japan*. Tokyo: Teikoku Shoin, 1957.

Trewartha, Glenn T. *Japan: A Physical, Cultural, and Regional Geography*. Madison and Milwaukee: University of Wisconsin Press, 1965.

Tsunoda, Ryusaku; de Bary, Wm. Theodore; and Keene,

Donald. *Sources of Japanese Tradition*. New York: Columbia University Press, 1958.

Vogel, Ezra. *Japan's New Middle Class*. Berkeley and Los Angeles: University of California Press, 1964.

Watsuji, Tetsuro. *A Climate: A Philosophical Study*. Tokyo: Government Printing Office, 1961.

BCL - 3rd ed